Torn
and
Broken

Torn
and
Broken

One woman's emotional journey of
finding herself and becoming whole again

CSILLA BATIZY SMITH

XULON PRESS

Xulon Press
2301 Lucien Way #415
Maitland, FL 32751
407.339.4217
www.xulonpress.com

Printed in the United States of America.

ISBN-13: 978-1-6305-0837-1

Dedication

I t is with love and gratitude that I dedicate this book to my children, Blake and Lenti, and my granddaughter, Margot Blake. You have inspired me to be a better person and to always strive to be the best I can be.

Also, to the memory of my mother and grandparents who loved me unconditionally.

To everyone who helped me throughout this journey.

Table Of Contents

Acknowledgements

Special thanks:

To my readers, may you find inspiration and hope in becoming the best you can be and finding peace in your life.

To Elaine, my lifelong friend, who stood beside me and helped me through the most difficult times in my journey.

To Karen, who encouraged me to write my story to inspire others in their quest to overcoming the hardships in their lives.

To Ron and all the people who "happened" in my life at precisely the right moment when I was lost, had nowhere to go, and in total despair.

To Kris, one of the many parents of students I taught who always showed her support and recognized my fight for every child in my care.

To Lou, one of the kindest, most caring, and thoughtful people I've ever known. Thank you for accepting me for who I am with no strings attached. Thank you for not allowing me to leave my story in the filing cabinet and pushing me to take this final step in getting my story out.

Introduction

After all these years, there it is again. That lump in my throat I felt many, many times before. I would always get that lump when someone asked me about my life. People would say, "Tell me about how you came to America. Aw, come on, tell me all about it." It's not that I was ashamed or didn't want to tell them, it's just that every time I tried to tell the story I would start crying. It was as if I was eight years old again and all those horrible feelings rushed back. It literally made me physically sick, so I would put them off by telling them that I would tell the story later, hoping that later would never come. This time, however, I had no choice. My children wanted to know and although I put them off for years, I finally agreed. It took the encouragement and support of my dear friends Elaine, Karen, and Lou to make it happen.

I started to chronicle my life's journey over two decades ago. My journey included war, being taken from my mother against my will, adjusting to being part of a dysfunctional blended family, learning a new language, and assimilating to the customs of a foreign land. Of course, these were difficult things to share with strangers. On top of all those hurdles, dealing with constant emotional and physical abuse was nearly unbearable to put in words. So, telling the actual journey to America wasn't the issue. The challenges that occurred during the escape and life in America throughout the years that followed, were nearly impossible to discuss. That is why I put off sharing my story until now.

I believe that all of us have it within ourselves to overcome whatever trauma is holding us back. Yes, the scars remain. We do not forget, but through it all, we become a better person and are able to help others in need. We are able to live in the present—the here and now— and are no longer held hostage by our past.

With that being said, I truly hope that by sharing my story you will find the courage to believe in yourself and move forward with your life. I did, you can too!

Today, I am a well-respected educator with over 39 years of teaching experience in the classroom. During those years, I taught all elementary grades except Grades 1 and 3. In the evenings, I taught adult education classes to help prepare those who were seeking their GED. The road to where I am now was long and hard. Every step was a struggle and an uphill climb. In the end, I not only had a wonderful career as a teacher, but I also had a private practice as a psychologist helping people overcome issues with alcohol and drug addiction, domestic violence, and shoplifting for over a decade. So, you might ask, "How did that little refugee girl coming to this country with only her clothes on her back get from there to where she is today?"

Here is my story.

Chapter 1

Gödöllö

I only lived in my homeland, Hungary, for a short period of time. I was 8 years old when we fled from our war-torn country in 1956. Although I lived in Budapest, some of my fondest memories are of being with my grandparents in Gödöllö. Gödöllö, in the 1950s, was a quiet, rural, farming community located approximately 16 miles east of Budapest. At that time, the roads in Gödöllö were unpaved and the only means of transportation from Budapest to Gödöllö was by train. In Budapest, we used the villamos (tram) to get from one location to another, but in Gödöllö all travel was by foot or horse and buggy. I believe I was about four years old when I started spending my summers there. To this day, I love the occasional thoughts that come to my mind of those visits. I smile each time I think about those lazy summer days.

My grandfather, who I called Nagypapi, was a farmer and I loved going out to the fields with him. While he worked the ground, I played in the dirt. When I got hungry, I pulled fresh vegetables out of the ground, wiped them off and ate them. If I close my eyes, I can still taste the carrots, tomatoes and other vegetables. At the end of the day, we made our way back to the house in nagypapi's

1

horse-drawn wagon which was pulled by his horse named Laci. Often I fell asleep during the ride home, and my nagypapi had to carry me into the house.

I loved everything about the farm. I loved the smell, the animals and even the outhouse. I looked forward to spending the summers there. Sometimes my sister would go with me and sometimes one of my brothers would be there, but there were never more than two of us in Gödöllö at a time. No matter who was there, it was always an adventure. It did not matter if we were playing with the pigs in the backyard or feeding corn to the hens, or collecting eggs in the early morning, it was a nice place to be. It was simple and beautiful!

I remember my sister Gyömbi and me playing in the yard with vegetables we picked from the field. We wanted to carve dolls out of them and dress them up in clothes we planned on making later. I'm not sure what went wrong, but the next thing I remember is throwing the vegetables in our well. "Hey," I told my sister, "these vegetables float! Oh no! What if someone finds out what we did?" I no more uttered those words when my great-grandmother, known to us as Szűle, appeared out of nowhere. "What are you girls doing?" she asked. I can't remember what happened next, except I do remember she came after us with her walking cane muttering something under her breath that was hard to understand. Of course, we didn't need to understand what she was saying. We already knew we were in big trouble and that we would be reported to our grandparents. Soon we would have to face the consequences of our behavior.

There were other times Szűle got after me. One day, out of the clear blue, I picked up a cat and swung it by its tail. I was a curious 8-year-old. Oh, did I get a thrashing for that! Of course, there were other misdeeds over the years, but I don't remember them all. The fact is, I felt loved on the farm not only by my grandparents but also by Szűle. She was a tough disciplinarian, but fair. She was my nagy-papi's mother and she lived with my grandparents. She had a one room studio apartment that was attached to my grandparents' house. I am sure my nagypapi built it for her when he built his house. It was an apartment with a separate entrance. I don't recall her having a kitchen or anything else in the room just a bed. During mealtimes, my nagymami fixed her a plate and one of us took it to her. She was always dressed in black and spent hours telling us stories. I loved hearing her talk about how things were when she was young. Some days though, she spent the whole time showing me the dress she wanted to be buried in at her funeral. I did not like those days at all. It upset me to even think of being on the farm and Szűle not being there. I just couldn't imagine what life would be like without her.

My one and only cousin, Mária, lived across the street from my grandparents. I remember playing with her and getting in trouble. Being young and carefree children, we managed to do that quite often. Perhaps it was because what one did not think of doing the other did! I remember on one particular occasion we were playing theater in the outhouse. Oh yes, we were quite creative and used the wooden platform as our stage. The odor did not seem to bother us, and we played for hours on top of hours laughing and having a good time. The last time we played theater was when I fell in. I guess my foot slipped and in I went. What a mess! What a terrible mess! Oh, and that smell! My nagymami had to bathe me outside so as to not get that horrible stench in the house. While she was washing me off, she told me that she was going to put me in a basket, put the basket on the light pole and send me home. I heard that same story many times whenever I misbehaved, but I was never sent home that way. Still, part of me was afraid that this time she would follow through. I couldn't take the chance!

Now as I think about it, what was it about the outhouse that attracted me to play there in the first place? Why was it that more than once I got in serious trouble because of that place? As I think back, I used it for more than just a playhouse. I also used it as a hiding spot. One morning I woke up with a craving for watermelon, but when I asked if I could have some, my nagypapi told me the watermelons were not ripe. It's not that I did not believe him, I just thought, maybe he was wrong since they looked ripe to me. As soon as the opportunity presented itself, I helped myself to a couple of melons. Yes, I even tapped on them like I saw my mother do when we went shopping for melons at the market. They sounded okay to me, but to my dismay, Nagypapi was right! The watermelons were not ready. As soon as I slammed them against the ground to open them up, I saw the insides were definitely not ripe. What was I to do? I had to get rid of the evidence, so I hid them in the outhouse. I threw them in the hole, put the lid down and didn't give it another thought. Certainly, I did not realize that my move to hide the evidence was at minimum foolish. The thought never occurred to me that the next person who entered the outhouse would see the melons that were apparently visible as soon as the lid was lifted, but I was still shocked when I was called to the house and got the basket lecture.

Like I said before, the whole basket thing did not make sense to me, but I wasn't taking any chances. Summer was not over yet, so I was not ready to go. I begged and pleaded with my nagymami not to send me back and besides, I would argue with her, how could I fit in the basket and how could the basket jump the poles in order for me to get to Budapest. My nagymami would just shake her head and give that particular look she so well knew how to give. I stopped arguing and pleading and believed if I did not straighten up, she would indeed send me back home. I would not only be sent back home, but I would also be traveling in a basket instead of taking the train to Budapest.

After all, if my nagymami said that is what was going to happen, it had to be true.

My nagymami was a beautiful woman. She was short in stature and had long hair which she wore in a bun on top of her head. At night, she took down her bun and brushed her long beautiful hair for what seemed like hours. I sat there watching her and thinking, "One day I, too, will have long beautiful hair like hers." My hair was short, parted on the side, and always with a big bow on the right side. All the girls I knew wore their hair that way. I was no different.

Although I enjoyed playing with my cousin I did not like being at her house. I was afraid to be around my aunt and spent as little time as possible there. I always knew she loved me, but when I was mischievous, which you already know was quite often, she took out her teeth and chased me around the room with them. She knew I was afraid of those teeth, but she took them out anyway. Actually, I'm sure that's why she took them out. My uncle, on the other hand, was the opposite of her. He played with us, told us stories and gave us sugar cubes for no reason at all. It was nice being around him and I looked forward to him coming across the street to visit his parents and me.

Every summer vacation was filled with great adventures; therefore, it made me sad for those magical summers to come to an end. I always knew when it was time to go back to Budapest. It was right after harvest. At the close of the summer I rode with my nagypapi to the marketplace where he sold his fruits and vegetables. Days later he took me to the train station where I took the train back to Budapest. Sometimes tears streamed down my face as I left the farm, and other times my eyes welled up with tears, but there were always tears. Although I loved my home, I also loved being with my grandparents. Little did I know that at the end of that particular summer I would never see my grandparents again and it would be decades before my cousin, and I would be reunited.

Until their death, each Christmas, birthday, or periodically for no special occasion, I received a note from them and enclosed in the envelope I would find a pressed flower. Those brief letters and flowers meant the world to me. They were an affirmation of their love for me and a tie to my past.

When my son, Blake, was born, I sent a birth announcement to my family in Hungary. I had no idea that the day they received the announcement was the day of my uncle's (their only son's) funeral. They were devastated and grief stricken by the death of their child, but later I found out that the birth announcement helped them through the grieving process.

My nagymami sent me a beautiful letter and shared the story of my uncle's tragic death writing, "God takes one love away and replaces that loved one with another." Enclosed with the letter was a pressed flower. To this day, I still have that flower. Each time I look at it, I think of my loving grandparents and my loving uncle, and it transports me back to the farm in Gödöllö.

My reunion with Mária was bittersweet. I returned to Hungary for my mother's funeral in 2000, and it was during this time that I saw her again. She and her husband lived in my grandparents' house and their child and spouse lived across the street in what was my aunt and uncle's house years ago. Although some modifications had been made to the house over the years, I recognized it easily. As we sat around the kitchen table, I allowed the memories to wash over me. When I closed my eyes, I could see my grandparents in the kitchen with us. They were home and so was I.

Blake and I with the pressed flower from Nagymami

Anyu, Nagypapi and Nagymami in Gödöllö

Blake and his cousin in my grandparents' house in 2000

Chapter 2

Life on Költö Utca

B udapest is the capital of Hungary and is well known for its beautiful architecture, history, bathhouses, and so much more, but as a small child, it was just home to me. The city is divided by the Danube River. On one side of the river is Pest, and on the other side is Buda. Buda is located on the hilly side of Budapest on the West Bank of the Danube. We lived in district XII on Szabadság Hegy (Freedom Hill) on Költö Utca. In the winters we skied on the mountain, and when warm weather arrived, we hiked on the hiking trails.

In my early years, I attended daycare and kindergarten at St. János Korház where Mother worked in the x-ray department. The only memory I have of those days is taking the villamos (tram) to and from the hospital. My brother Zsolt, however, has shared numerous stories with me over the years about things that happened in kindergarten. To me, they were only stories. I could never make any connection to them no matter how hard I tried over the years to recall those incidents.

One of the things he's repeatedly told me over the years was how one day a bunch of kids ganged up on me, for no reason at all, and beat me up. He proudly recalled how he came to my rescue and saved me from those kids. According to him, the teacher just stood there and watched the kids wailing on me without doing anything to stop the fight. He often suggested that the teacher enjoyed the fight. Although I've repeatedly thanked him for saving me, I still, to this day, do not remember any of it. Maybe it is one of those repressed memories that will eventually come to light. Until then, I will just continue to smile and say, "Thank you," to him for saving me from that terrible ordeal—real or imagined.

Once I was old enough to start school, I attended the elementary school that was about one or two blocks from our apartment. Grades 1 through 3 only attended school half a day while the other grades went full day. My favorite grade was first grade. My teacher was young and funny, and I loved her. There were many days I sat at my desk and thought about becoming a teacher just like her. I wish she lived long enough, so I could have thanked her for inspiring me to become a teacher, but that wasn't to be. Not long after we were in the States, I received a letter from my mother stating that she died of cancer. I cried and cried.

Thoughts of that special teacher came back to me many years later when I received a phone call from a colleague of mine to let me know that on the first day of school in a faculty meeting her principal asked his teachers to say who inspired and impacted their lives the most. One by one the faculty members recalled the educator who had the greatest impact on their lives. At the end, the principal shared his story of the person who inspired him to become an educator. He told the story of his 6th grade teacher who escaped from Hungary in 1956. He said this teacher not only influenced him to become a teacher, but also to study history and become a history teacher—it came full circle. I helped mold this person's life just like my 1st grade teacher molded mine.

A few days after that telephone call, my good friend Em sent me a text to let me know she had just left the memorial service of a former student of mine who had been killed in Afghanistan and that I was mentioned in the service. When his mother spoke during his service, she mentioned her son's love for his kindergarten teacher. Em felt it was important for me to know how I touched this person's life. This was the reason I became a teacher. I wanted to show love and support to all my students, and to positively impact their lives just like my teacher in Hungary influenced my life.

I had just started third grade when the uprising in 1956 broke out; therefore, I only have a few recollections of that school year. Like I said before, I do remember that I loved going to school even though there were times I felt my teacher did not like me. I, being the fifth child out of my parents' six children, I am afraid that for whatever reason my teacher had all she could stand of the Batizy children. I tried hard in school and did not understand the politics of teaching, so it was hard for me to understand why my teacher did not like me. Maybe it was because one time when she left the room I got out of my seat and walked up on the platform, stood in front of her desk and tried to entertain my classmates by pretending to be the teacher. And, oh yes, when one of my classmates said something to me I didn't like I turned around, bent over and told him to kiss the monkey's behind. You can imagine how shocked I was when I turned back around and saw my teacher standing there. She took me by my braids and directed me back to my seat. I knew I would pay for that bit of clowning around once at home. The next morning when Dad came for his visit, he lit into me like there was no tomorrow once he read the note and learned what I had done. My father was old school. If you got in trouble at school, you got in trouble at home. Oh, did I ever! It seemed like an hour or longer before I was able to sit down again. My bottom was sore!

We wore uniforms to school, and I was a junior pioneer. I wore my navy skirt and white blouse proudly with my blue scarf tied neatly around my neck. By the end of third grade, I knew I would get to exchange the blue scarf for a red one and get to do some of the things that being a pioneer allowed. I would get to drive the pioneer train, and my parents would be so proud of me. I soon found out that my parents wanted no part of the red scarf which they said was a corner of the Russian flag and any and all discussions about me becoming a pioneer and driving the train was to stop immediately. Now, all my excitement had to be kept a secret. I knew I would do whatever it took to drive the train. I dreamt about it every day.

There were times I felt my 3rd grade teacher did not like me. On those occasions I sat in class wishing I was one of my classmates who everybody knew the teacher adored. As I sat there, I told myself, "If I were her then someone would be sitting where I was sitting, and they would be sad. So, it is okay, I can handle being me."

Looking back, I was a good kid and a decent student. I tried to do as I was asked and other than talking too much in class and an occasional mishap, I did not get in trouble. I did not have the photographic mind of my sister Gyömbi, but I did okay when I studied and applied myself. There were times when studying was not first on my to do list. Dad always held us accountable for our grades and made sure our schoolwork was complete. I hated for him to work with me on any school assignment. He was short on patience and did not mind spanking or hitting me when I recited the wrong answer. I could not relax with him, and the harder I tried not to make a mistake the more mistakes I made. My father was short tempered and abusive to his family. I dreaded every visit.

One day when I heard my father in our apartment, I hid so he couldn't find me. I was not in the mood for lectures on stupidity and how my siblings were better students than me. I guess, to him, he was trying to motivate me, but to me it was an affirmation of how I was not as good as they were, so I hid. I was extremely small for my age and I hid in the bed which was not made up at the time. I lay under the comforter as still as I could and hoped and prayed, he would not find me. I heard him and Valika looking for me, but soon Dad had to leave, and I emerged out of bed acting like I just woke up. I was spared a "beating" that day or at minimum an inevitable back hand to the face. Oh, how I hated those.

In 1954 my parents divorced. I don't remember my father ever living in our home, but none-the-less, my parent's divorce did not become final until 1954. Dad already lived with my stepmother and their children. I heard my grandmother Valika and my mother talking about it, but as a small child, I did not know what to make of the different things I heard. I didn't understand that once the divorce was final, and my dad finally married my stepmother, certain things would happen to cause our happy home, as we knew it, to change forever. Dad had always paid child support and also gave Mom additional money for his mother, Valika. This changed as soon as he remarried. He cut his support down to only what the courts ordered him to pay and thus created a situation where he was able to pressure Mom into letting my three brothers live with him. Financially Mom was not able to provide for their six children and her mother-in-law on what she was receiving in child support even with her salary, so reluctantly she allowed my brothers to go live with Dad. Dad wanted all the children, but Mom kept us girls with her. This arrangement would change later.

But let's focus on happier times. As I mentioned, my mother, Valika, my brothers, sisters and I lived on Költö Utca on the Buda side of Budapest. We lived in a one-bedroom apartment on the second floor. The communist/socialist government dictated the size of the apartment a family could occupy. Today it seems like it should have been a tight squeeze with all eight of us sleeping in one room, but back then it seemed perfectly normal. My two sisters and I slept in one of the twin beds, and my three brothers slept in the twin bed located at the foot of my mother and Valika's double bed. Our bedroom was where we did everything. The living room was only used for company and the kitchen was mostly for meals. That left just the bedroom where we played and played and played when it was too cold to play outside, or if it was raining, or for whatever reason we could not go out.

On those cold wintry days, the windows of our bedroom became our canvases. We loved to draw and paint, and we painted on the windows every chance we had. It's funny now but I remember years later letting my 6th grade students paint on the windows in my classroom at Mt. Juliet Elementary School. It was a rare treat for them, and they always seemed to enjoy that experience as much as I did years earlier as a young child in Hungary. I even divided the class into two teams like we used to do, and we had a contest as to who had the best painting. The only difference being that instead of mother and Valika judging the paintings, I was the one doing the judging. The prize was not the coveted sugar cube as in Hungary, but a real piece of candy like a Tootsie Roll or maybe a Now-or-Later. Each student of the winning team received the prize!

We knew how to entertain ourselves and each other on Költö Utca, so we were never bored. We always had something to do. One night while my mother and Valika went out for coffee, we decided to put on a ballet performance. Before you knew it, we had ballerina costumes made of t-shirts, and we were dancing all over the room. Our imaginations were unstoppable, and we never ran out of ideas of things to do. It was so much fun. We danced and danced until we could dance no more.

On other occasions we put on plays in the kitchen. The radiator was our stage. We took turns getting on top of the radiator and performing. We spent hours laughing and having fun. One night my sister Gyömbi slipped and cut her leg right above the knee. There was blood everywhere. Our acting quickly turned to playing doctor and bandaging her up. With our parents being doctors, medical supplies were always on hand. When Anyu (Mother) and Valika came home, we were in trouble and we knew it. We were always told to take care of each other, and one of us getting hurt was not acceptable. Not only was it not acceptable, but we knew we were not supposed to be playing in the kitchen in the first place. From that point on, the radiator was off limits to us, and we stayed out of the kitchen except for mealtimes. Oh yes, I grew up in a family where spanking was in style. No misdeed was ever overlooked, and we all got our fair share of discipline. The older ones, it seemed got more since the mindset of our parents was that the older children should have known better. At those times, I was thankful I was the baby girl of the family.

We also played for hours with paper dolls. We drew our own dolls and, also, designed their dresses and costumes. Each outfit was more elegant than the one before. Not only did the girls play with paper dolls but my brothers did also. Their dolls weren't pretty or dainty; they made paper soldiers with guns. That was a contrast to what my sisters and I created. It was fun none-the-less and brings back such pleasant memories.

On rainy days and nights, we enjoyed playing board games and chess. I don't know when I learned to play chess. Perhaps I was born knowing how or perhaps my siblings taught me. All I know is, that by age eight, I was an excellent chess player. Of course, I was. I had to be good in order to get to play with my older brothers and sisters. No one wanted to play with a baby.

One morning we woke to loud rumbling and the furniture moving across the room. Even the chandelier was swaying back and forth. It was really scary. I didn't know what was happening. My sister Gyömbi told me it was an earthquake. It didn't take long for my brothers to say that the earth was going to open up and swallow our building. I must have been a real scaredy-cat for I still remember being afraid. What else was going to happen? I knew right then and there that it was the end of us. I just knew we were gone for sure. Yes, we survived the earthquake, and life was back to normal within a few hours. There was no damage to our building, and other than being scared, we were fine. Valika was there to hold and comfort us.

My grandmother Valika was a widow and always lived with us. She did not want to be called grandmother though. She preferred to be called by her nickname, Valika, which is short for Valeria. She was born into privilege with linkage to royalty that dates back to 1265. The family, however, lost all their money after World War I when the currency of Hungary changed, but her breeding and upbringing was passed down to our generation. It was her duty to make sure we were exposed to the finer things in life such as the opera, musicals, plays, and such.

My first and last musical as a child was called "Három a Kis Lány." Valika took the three girls, which, of course, was appropriate since the title of the musical translated to English as "The Three Little Girls." We were all dressed in our white sailor suits which she sewed for us, and all three of us sported a big beautiful dark blue bow in our hair. I felt extra special since this was my first musical and only the girls got to go. Valika was great. I'm so glad she decided to stay with us to help Mom. She wanted to make sure her grandchildren were taken care of and raised well. After all, Mother was now a single working mom trying to take care of six children.

Like his mother, my father tried to instill in us a pride for where we came from. He, not only, wanted us to be proud of our heritage, but he also wanted us to know our roots. On his 75th birthday he wrote a letter to each of his children giving us information about our ancestors. I am still amazed at our family tree and am so proud to be a Batizy even though being a Batizy had its price. It was because of my heritage that the family had to leave Hungary during the 1956 uprising. My father paid for his father's political affiliation by officially being blacklisted by the ruling communist party during the cold war era.

In his letter, father shared the following story with each of us. Interestingly enough, this was the first time I heard any mention of my grandfather Batizy. My grandfather, Dr. Gusztáv Batizy, was a Budapest Police Commissioner who died from a botched kidney surgery at age 44. My father was only 14 years old at the time of his death. The family's lineage reaches back to the founding days of the Hungarian Reformed Church. András Batizy was born in 1510. He was one of the founders of the Hungarian Reform Church. He was also a bishop, translator of the Bible, and published author. One of his poems written in 1546 is still famous today. The title of that poem is "Régi Ének a Hazasságrol." Another family member who held an important position was István Batizy. He was a heroic officer in the artillery unit of the Rákoczi tribe in the 18th century. His son, Márton Batizy was affiliated with the Hungarian Reform Church. Márton and his wife had four children. One of his children was Dr. János Batizy, who grew up to be Dean of Law at the University. He was my great, great grandfather. His son, Dr. Gusztáv Batizy, was my great grandfather. I do not know too much about him except that he married the daughter of the Mayor of Szölnök and they had five children.

Although Dad did not live with us, we saw him all the time. I want to say we saw him probably every day, but that may not be so. That is just the memory I have. Dad would come up and visit us and go over our homework. If the homework was not up to his standards, we were ridiculed and often physically punished. Other times he would come up and take us swimming, skiing, or hiking. He was into sports. Oh, I almost forgot, we even did gymnastics. I don't think there was a sport we were not introduced to as children. I remember the three things Dad emphasized to us:

1. Have pride in your heritage

2. Get a good education

3. The importance of sports

It was during those sporting events that I saw and got to spend time with my half-brothers and later my own brothers as well.

I have many memories of various trips the family took with Dad. The first one was when Dad took us to Lake Balaton one summer. We had a rowboat named "Testvériség" which means brotherhood in English. On one particular outing, we got caught in a huge thunderstorm. We quickly took to shore on a small island, and I remember all of us huddled under our boat which Dad turned upside down to give us shelter. Even with the lightening and the fierce storm, I felt safe surrounded by my family. We prayed for safety, and I knew we were going to be all right, and we were!

Dad taught all of us to swim. I am not sure how old I was when it was my turn to learn. I am sure I was way too young. I was perfectly content to stay in the baby pool. I do remember my brothers and sisters "learning" to swim, and I wanted no part of that process. Every day when we went to the pool. I dreaded it. I knew the time was coming very soon when it would be my turn. And then that fated day came when Dad told me to jump in the water and swim to him. Of course, he reassured me that he would be there to keep me safe. I refused and didn't move from the edge of that pool. Didn't Dad know I did not know how to swim? As Dad gave the command, one of my brothers pushed me into the pool. When I came up for air, I was crying and screaming that I could not swim. Dad kept saying he was there and for me to swim to him, but I saw what he was doing. I saw him moving backwards and I was never able to quite reach him. The more he moved the harder I cried. I screamed and kicked until finally I miraculously reached the other side of the pool. I could hardly wait to go home and tell Mom I knew how to swim. Surely that night I would get a sugar cube for a job well done!

Yes, Dad stayed in contact with his first family, but it is important to acknowledge that every visit was hardly fun and games. Too often, I witnessed his abusive relationship with his own mother. On those days, I hid from my father. As a young child I didn't know what triggered the arguments that escalated to physical violence, but I knew that I had to protect myself and hide. I put myself in survival mode. It became a default.

Right before the uprising, Dad took us skiing. Of course, I knew how to ski. I was 8 years old and had been skiing for years. Skiing, ice skating, we did it all. Dad made sure we were physically fit. On that day there was a man at the slopes taking pictures of people skiing. Although we did not know anything about him, later we found out he was a photographer for a magazine. He took my picture standing there with my skis in my hand getting ready for a fun filled day on the slopes. A year later that random picture appeared on the cover of a magazine giving my mother a near heart attack as she was trying to find out where I was. But I am getting ahead of myself.

Picture of me taken right before the revolution

The girls in our sailor suits made by Valika

Our family in Hungary

Chapter 3

Revolution

The Hungarian people, under the communist regime, did not have religious freedom. Families literally disappeared because of their faith and church attendance. For that reason, we did not attend church in Hungary, but my mother and Valika taught us to pray early in life. We recited the Lord's Prayer every night at bedtime which I still do to this day. Shortly before the uprising, as I was going home from school, I was drawn to go inside the Catholic Church that was visible from our school. I remember going in and seeing the beauty of it all. I was in awe and stayed for quite some time. When I left the church, it was already dark outside, and I got turned around and got lost. It was extremely late when I got home. I recall getting in trouble for not coming straight home from school, and, of course, I got the lecture of what could happen if anyone saw me coming out of a church, and reported the incident to the government just to receive an extra loaf of bread. Those were desperate times!

Days later, on October 23, 1956, fighting broke out in my country. Since then, I learned that the Hungarian Revolution of 1956 was a nationwide revolt against the Soviet Union. The people of Hungary wanted their freedom! The uprising began as a student demonstration

which attracted thousands as they marched through central Budapest
to the Parliament building. The Revolution only lasted nineteen days
from October 23 until November 10, 1956. During those nineteen
days there was a period that the Hungarians thought they gained
their freedom from the Soviet Union. The fighting virtually ceased
between October 28th and November 4th. I heard in early November
about negotiations and talk of Soviet withdrawal from our country.
There were many celebrations during that time. We were finally free!
This, however, was not to be. Instead, on November 4, 1956 large
Soviet forces invaded Budapest and other regions of Hungary. This
invasion did not stop the people and the fighting continued until
November 10th when the revolution officially ended, and the Soviets
were declared victors.

I saw many tanks coming and going on my street during this time.
This was not much different from what I was used to seeing all my
life. After World War II the Soviet military occupied Hungary and
gradually replaced the freely elected government with the Hungarian
Communist Party which used intimidation, false accusations, imprisonment, torture, and execution to suppress political opposition. The
communist government controlled every aspect of everyone's life.
Food was rationed, hot water was turned on only once a week, the
government even dictated the size of the home you lived in and its
location. This is what I grew up in, and I was taught early in life never
to repeat anything I heard at home.

During the revolution when the sirens sounded, the whole apartment complex went to the basement of the apartment building. We
listened to Radio Free Europe. There was chatter of families disap-
pearing. We prayed out loud for our safety, the safety of our friends,
and for our country. The entire apartment complex prayed together.
Everyone was reciting the Lord's Prayer. I was scared and wanted
things to go back to the way they were before the revolution broke

26

out. What I didn't know at that time was that my life would be changed forever, and it would never be the same again.

Dad and his second family lived in downtown Budapest on Dezsö Tér along with my brothers, Csaba, Levente, and Zsolt. My brothers went to live with Dad shortly before the revolution broke out. The girls stayed with Mother and Valika, but my father was determined to get all his children which included me. Dad's apartment was right across from the parliament building and the radio station on the other side of the Danube River on the Pest side of Budapest. His medical practice (office) was also in downtown Budapest within walking distance of where he and his family lived. This put him and his second family in grave danger when the revolution broke out. Additionally, Dad was a member of the Revolutionary Council. This meant that by November 1956 when the Russians crushed the Hungarian revolt, Dad risked imprisonment for ten years or even a death sentence by staying in Hungary. To protect his family, Dad made the decision to leave Hungary.

Early one morning, Mother got word of Dad's botched escape. She was notified by the government of his death. As the story was told, he and others dove into the Danube River when they were surrounded by the Russian soldiers in an attempt to escape capture and the likelihood of public hanging. Bullets were flying everywhere with some being killed and others wounded. The Russians assumed Dad was killed when his white doctor's coat with his ID floated to the surface. A funeral service was held for dad, but we did not attend. Instead, we were eagerly awaiting the return of our brothers to our home. That, of course, never happened. Before long, we realized that my father not only managed to escape to Austria, but he also snuck back into our country to get his children.

This is the church I visited as a child

Inside of that church I saw as a child

Russian tanks patrolling our streets

Chapter 4

Torn From Home

One night in late December I was awaked by loud voices. Mother was working at the hospital that night, so who was Valika arguing with? I suddenly recognized the two voices. Valika was arguing with my father. How can this be? We were told Dad was killed by the Russians during his attempted escape from capture. The argument was about him wanting to take the girls. He was determined to take us with him. I didn't want to go. As I lay in bed with my sister, I pulled the blanket over my head. At some point, I peeked out from under the covers and my eye caught a glimpse of our beloved picture that hung on the wall across from our bed. This picture was special to me since it was a picture of six angels, and Mother had six children. From time to time we each claimed one of the angels as our guardian. As I looked at the picture, I quietly said, "God, please don't make me go." Suddenly, Valika interrupted my prayer and hastened me to get dressed and told me that the family was leaving for America. "No," I said as tears began to form, I do not want to go," but I was taken away just the same.

Dad took us out of our bed in the middle of the night. He stole us from our mother. He kidnapped us and was taking us to America.

Why couldn't I stay like my sister Tűnde? She was the oldest, and for whatever reason she did not have to go. Years later I heard my siblings talking about the reason Tűnde didn't go with us. Come to find out, it was for her safety. Since Tűnde was a teenager, my father worried she would attract attention. He feared of what would happen to her if we were captured. Still to this day, I don't think it was fair. I wanted to stay. I did not want to go, but because I was only 8 years old, I was forced to leave the only life I knew and everyone and everything I loved.

That fateful night, I wore the sailor dress Valika made for me for my very first musical, and before I left, Valika combed my hair for the last time and placed a beautiful dark blue bow in my hair. I walked out the door with my father, and in that instant, my whole life changed forever.

Once we left Költö Utca we headed to my father's apartment in downtown Budapest. There the rest of the family met us, and we were on our way. Dad gave us lots of instructions. He said, "Do not speak to anyone." He also told us that, if we were stopped, to say we were on our way to visit our sick grandparents. We were told to call my stepmother "Mama," and at that moment we became one family. She became our mother. The train ride to the outskirts of Budapest was long. Dad, my stepmother and the eleven children must have been a sight traveling in the middle of the night. It didn't matter how often Dad reminded us to not draw attention to ourselves, we no more stepped off the train when the family was surrounded by Russian soldiers with their rifles pointed at us. We did not say a word and stood there while Dad spoke to them in Russian. He told them the story about where we were going, but for whatever reason, they did not believe him. We were taken to a Red Cross station which served as a prisoner of war camp. This is where we stayed until a decision was made as to what they would do with us. The place was full of people.

I listened carefully as people talked around me. I heard stories that my father and stepmother would be taken to Siberia and all the children (not just Mother's five children) would be returned to Budapest. What great news! I would be going home. I could not

think about what would happen to my father and stepmother, I could only think about going home and being with my mother. Oh, and getting to see the picture on the wall in our bedroom—the picture of the six angels that comforted me all throughout my life that I had to leave behind when father took us away that night. Soon my happy thoughts were interrupted by something my father was saying. I put my hands over my ears. I did not want to hear of another escape plan. I did not want to leave my home. I did not want to leave. I prayed, "God, please don't let him take me."

Early next morning we were told to get dressed for a farewell dinner. It was Christmas Eve and Dad and my stepmother got permission from the Russian soldiers to take the children out to eat before we were sent back to Budapest. I felt that God answered my prayer. I was going home. I had an extra kick in my step as I headed out the door for our last meal together.

No, this cannot be. Something is terribly wrong. We walked past the restaurant, and we kept walking and walking. I tried to speak, but Dad made me hush. What is happening? Where are we going? These were the questions that were running through my mind, but I dared not say them aloud. Dad said, "Hush," and I did not want to get in trouble. As we walked on, there were no answers to my questions. Soon it became obvious that we were not going to stop for our last dinner together. We were heading toward what was unknown to me. I finally accepted the fact that I was not going home in less than 24 hrs.

As we walked, the little town we left grew smaller and smaller in the distance. We just kept moving. Before long we were in the middle of nowhere. We trudged through knee deep snow toward the unknown. Somewhere out there in the dark beyond the barbed wire, the watchtowers, and the machine guns was Austria and freedom. All of us were hungry, cold and tired, but we kept going just the same. There was no turning back. At times we joined hands to help each other as we made our way through the snow and thick woods. Later we lay on the ground in an irrigation ditch when we heard voices. Though I did not know it at that time, on the other side of that ditch was freedom. This time we were lucky. There were no bullets to dodge, the watch towers were dark, and there was no one patrolling that particular spot. The way was clear!! What else was clear was the fact that I was not going home. I would not see my mother or grandparents again. I was no one's little Csilike. I was just one of eleven kids heading somewhere far, far away where I did not want to be. I would have cried, but I was too tired, hungry and scared for tears, coupled with the fear of being physically punished for crying. Crying was not allowed!

By the time we reached Austria it was very late at night. As people walked by us on the street, Father stopped and chatted with them. He asked for directions as to where the closest refugee camp was located. They would point in various directions, and we followed those instructions as if we were sheep being led to slaughter. Finally, we were there. We reached a refugee camp where we stayed until a decision was made as to where we would go. We were given food, a place to sleep and fresh clothes. Since it was Christmas, someone gave us some toys. Sure, people were nice, but someone took my sailor suit my Valika made for me. Someone cut my hair and my bow was gone. Everything I loved was gone. I was on my own. I wanted to go home. I wanted my mother, my grandmother and my sister Tűnde. I told my stepmother I wanted to go home, but I soon learned that what I wanted did not matter, and what I thought was not to be spoken. I was to do as I was told with no questions asked. And that is how my new life began.

Dad wanted to leave Austria as quickly as possible. He knew communist agents had been known to kidnap one member of a family and blackmail the others to return to Hungary. Arrangements were made by I.R.C. (International Red Cross) to move the family. From Austria we were taken to Germany to a US Army Base.

When we arrived in Germany there were photographers everywhere, and the headlines in the newspaper the next day read, "Eleven Children..." They lined us up from oldest to youngest. We were told to smile and then came the flashbulbs. My father was very proud of his family, and everywhere we went, we attracted attention. Even back in those days having eleven children was considered a large family coupled with my father's story of how he escaped from Hungary and snuck back into the country to get his children was something people wanted to read about. It certainly was the feel-good story of the time, but in reality, he was a father in name only. He was verbally, emotionally, and physically abusive.

We did not stay in Germany long, but while we were there, we lived on base. During that time, there was a search for someone to sponsor our family. It was the job of the sponsor to pay the cost of our transportation to the United States. The sponsor also had to have a place for us to live once we arrived. I heard Father talking about this, but I really did not understand any of it. I was more interested in building forts out of snow and having snowball fights and battles with my brothers.

The American Soldiers spoiled us by giving us candy bars and this sticky pink chewy stuff that was hard to swallow. At first, we did not like it. We never had bubble gum before and did not know what it was. We thought it was candy. The Soldiers laughed at us as we were trying to eat the "candy" they gave us, but eventually one of them showed us what to do with it. They taught us how to blow bubbles. What fun! Little did I realize that the assimilation process had begun.

We also learned our first few words of English in Germany. We learned the words chocolate, and gum and we were not too shy to say those words to anyone who would listen. Often, we were rewarded for our efforts with a candy bar or with gum. At times we got both. Other times the soldiers would give us money. We learned to recognize the dollar and its value. It, too, was added to our vocabulary. If I remember correctly, we asked for chocolate and gum first, and if we got the shake of the head indicating no, we quickly asked for a dollar. Life was very different.

I think the soldiers enjoyed us as much as we enjoyed being there with them, but as with everything else, a sponsor was found, and we were on our way to the United States. A Presbyterian Church in Chicago, Illinois decided to sponsor the family. It was time to go. Once more everything that people had given us was left behind. The few toys that were given to us over the Christmas holidays were gone. Also gone were the articles of clothing we were given. Once more, everything was taken away just like my sailor suit and my beautiful dark blue bow. Our family was going to American leaving everything behind.

Making our way to the U.S.A.

Chapter 5

Broken In America

The trip to the airport was both exciting and scary. I didn't know what to expect since I've never flown before, but I was not afraid. It was just something I had to do. In this relatively short period of time, I learned quickly to adapt to any situation. No one cared to hear about how I felt about things. There were too many children, and everyone was expected to do what they were told. I was no longer the next to the youngest of six children, and the baby girl. I was the fifth child of eleven in the States, or the sixth child if we were counting my oldest sister who was not with us. Since I was a girl, I had to help with the younger children. I became an instant babysitter for my younger siblings. I don't recall minding this added responsibility. Eventually, I learned there were perks that came with taking care of my sibs. One of the perks was that once in a blue moon my loyalty and hard work was rewarded with a new dress from Sears. More often than not, this reward would appear when my sister Gyömbi got in trouble.

I enjoyed the flight. The stewardesses, as they were called back then, were very nice, and we were waited on and pampered the whole trip. It was almost like being home with Anyu (Mother) and

Valika. I secretly thought of them all the time. I thought about not only them, but our apartment, my special picture, my friends, and my classmates I would never see again. At some point during the trip, I fell asleep. As the airplane approached the airport in Newark, New Jersey, I woke up. When we got off the plane there were more photographers. Everyone was anxious to see the family who escaped with eleven children.

Within minutes the family was whisked away, and we headed for Camp Kilmer in New Jersey. The reception center was operated by both military and civilian personnel. I was used to seeing soldiers. I have seen them all my life, so nothing about this seemed strange. Kilmer served as the processing center for all the Hungarian refugees. This was part of what was called the resettlement process. The State Department called this program as "Operation Safe Haven" and Kilmer itself had the nickname of "Operation Mercy." The steps to resettlement were of no interest to me. I was tired of medical check-ups, being finger printed, photographed, immunized and all the other stuff that went along with being new to this country. I wanted to go home—wherever that was.

Our next stop was Chicago, Illinois. The downtown YMCA was our home for a few days. What fun we had! We became collectors of tiny bars of soap. Every time we saw someone from the housekeeping service, we rushed her and asked for "SOUP!" At first the ladies just looked at us and shook their heads, but before long, they figured out what our hearts' desire was. We wanted their bars of soap. They gave us a few bars, but that wasn't enough. We were serious collectors and wanted more. Any cart left unattended became our targets. We went from floor to floor looking for soap. Before long we had a large supply. Each night we counted, stacked, and showed off our prized possessions. Although I was not the winner of having the most bars, I came in a close second and was very proud of myself.

One day we decided to make a swimming pool out of the shower stall. We covered the drain in one of the shower stalls and started running the water. We figured we could get in our pool from the top by climbing on a chair and scaling the glass shower door that did not completely reach the top. What a letdown and how disappointing it was to find out that instead of a pool we got a spanking for flooding the room and the rooms on the floor below us. I, of course, like all my brothers and my sister, had no knowledge of who did it, or who even thought of doing such a thing. Late that night we talked about what happened, and we fell asleep trying to figure out what went wrong with our plan. The stall had a glass door on it, and it should have held the water. Who would have thought it would leak and cause such a mess.

We left the YMCA with our collection of soap and our memories. In retrospect, I am sure the manager was happy to see us go. In a few days we managed to not only flood his hotel but depleted his supply of soap as well. I guess he was thinking good riddance, although, he was courteous and smiled as we left. Recently I had the privilege of attending one of my nephew's wedding which took place in Chicago. Who would have guessed that the YMCA where we stayed decades ago would be within walking distance of our hotel? Yes, before we left Chicago to return home, each of us went by that YMCA. We took pictures and went down memory lane of all that transpired there so many years ago.

We started school immediately. What a strange experience that proved to be. The school, the classrooms, everything was so different from my school in Hungary. At home, girls and boys were not in the same classroom. We wore uniforms. The desks were bolted to the floor. I was in third grade in Budapest, but now I was in first grade again! I was shocked! Why did they put me in a room with a bunch of babies? What was going on? That had to be a mistake. All of us, my brothers and my sister and I were in first grade and all of us were in the same room. Is this what schools were like in the United States?

I am not sure who came up with this idea, but at some point, we started taking rolls of toilet paper home from school. The tissue was much softer than what we had at home. We used regular paper. Any paper that was no longer needed was crumbled up and used as toilet tissue. Why is it that no matter how much the paper was crumbled, it was never as soft as what we found at school? And yes, one day, we decided to take some home. Our next big find was reams of paper we found in a closet next to the bathroom. I have no idea what we were doing in the closet, but we found paper, and we were thrilled. They had so much, and we were always on the lookout for drawing paper. We hit the jackpot!

We left school each day with an arm full of things we found. My stepmother always asked where we were getting the stuff and we simply replied, "We found them." She said that when we find something it is ours to keep. And, so, for a while, we kept finding more and more things. One day, someone at school stopped us as we were heading out the door. They looked at us and said, "No!" By that time, we had added that word to our vocabulary, and we knew we had done something wrong. They took our reams of paper, and we could not explain to them that it was ours. We found them! Besides that, we learned many years before in a faraway land that pioneers do not steal, they acquire.

As we went to and from school, whenever we saw a person on the street, we would ask them for a dollar. More often than not, we got the dollar we asked for. Also, by this time, we learned that coke bottles could be taken back to the store, and we could get money for them. We became collectors of coke bottles, and we were not bashful to ask for money on top of that. After all, this was America, and everyone had dollars. We looked at each person as being a millionaire.

Since we did not speak English, school was not important to us. Our parents sent us to school every morning, but on our way to school we would get distracted. Sometimes we would play on the playground instead of going to class. Other times we would look for coke bottles, and then, there were times we just took our sweet time getting to school. Often, we showed up to school late. On the days when collecting bottles made us late, we'd drag into class with several bottles under our arms. Our teacher would shake her head in disbelief. I don't know which annoyed her more, the fact that we were late, or that we brought those dirty bottles into her room. At first, she tried to take the bottles away from us, but after a while she gave up. Those were our bottles, and we were not about to share them with her. If she wanted bottles, she would have to look for them herself. And that is how our days at school went.

I recall another time when we returned to school late from lunch, our teacher was frustrated and angry with us and demanded to know why we were late. From her tone of voice and her gestures we knew we were in big trouble. Quickly, my brother started biting his arm and making barking noises and running around the room. Our excuse for being late was a dog chasing us and biting us. I don't think our teacher bought into our charade. She was visibly upset with us for once more disrupting her class. Our classmates, on the other hand, thought the whole thing was funny. Their laughter, I'm sure, was heard throughout the whole school.

Somehow, we discovered the dime store that was on our way to school. We hung out at that store every day and marveled at the things they were selling. I was particularly fascinated with two things. What caught my eye was the water guns that came in a variety of colors and the heart shaped manicure sets that had those cute little scissors, nail files and other things. They were a must-have for me. I grew impatient trying to save up enough money to make my purchase. Besides, just me having a water gun was not good enough. My brothers and sister had to have one too in order for us to be able to play army. What a pickle I found myself in. Oh, what to do! I knew that even if I acquired those items, I could not take them home. My stepmother would question me as to where they came from. Before long I had a plan. I would plant the items under a bush close to the house and accidentally find them on my way back from school. My brothers and sister would be witnesses to my great fortune. It was difficult, but I took the merchandise from the store and hid them in the bush close to the house. The guns were acquired first, and everyone was delighted at my find. We quickly divided the spoils and headed into the house. When questioned about where the guns came from, I quickly stepped forward and told her I found them adding that I had witnesses. I thought to myself, this is so easy. Tomorrow I will get two manicure sets. I knew Gyömbi would like one too.

I barely slept that night. As I closed my eyes, I could see the red, heart shaped manicure sets. Oh, if only it could be morning already, and I could go to the store to pick them up. And sure, as I am sitting here, I picked up the two manicure sets the next day and hid them under the same bush where the guns were the day before. On our way home from school, I miraculously found them. My brothers were envious of my good fortune. This time I didn't have to say anything when we got home since one of my brothers ran into the house and announced that I was the luckiest person alive. "Csilla found two manicure sets in the bushes," one of my brothers said. I smiled to myself, but before I knew it, that smile disappeared. I did not get to keep the manicure sets, but instead, I was questioned and accused of stealing. Although I insisted, I found the stuff to keep myself from getting in trouble, I was not believed and suffered the punishment that was dealt me. How could this be? The rules changed! Until now we were taught that anything found was ours to keep. As I got my spanking for stealing and lying, I reminded myself, "A pioneer does not steal. A pioneer acquires." From that point on, we were not allowed to keep anything we found, and I never stole again.

When school finally closed for the summer, we spent our days swimming in Lake Michigan every day. It was nice to get up in the mornings, do our chores and walk down to the beach. We became the "Swimming Batizys" and when we were not swimming, as I have stated earlier, we were collecting soda bottles. The beach was a perfect place for that. We collected and we saved. Finally, we had enough money to make our big purchases. We bought roller skates. Our skates were the kind that you attached to your shoes. We skated everywhere. We'd skate to the lake. We'd skate to the park. Wherever we went we skated. Those were such carefree days until something terrible happened.

Swimming in Lake Michigan was something we really enjoyed. At least until we saw a man drown. We told Dad what we saw, but he didn't believe us. We wanted out of the water. He said, "NO." It was not until the ambulance showed up and the lifeguard kept blowing his whistle that we were finally allowed to get out of the water. We saw the man being pulled from the lake, and it terrified me. The image of the man being worked on by the paramedics haunted me. It made me sick to see what they were doing to him. The man's stomach inflated like a balloon from the oxygen they pumped into him. It was a horrible sight that I could not get out of my head. I was afraid to even go to bed at night. I just knew the dead man was under my bed. I don't know where those thoughts came from, but I knew he was there. Every night before I climbed into my bed, I looked under the bed to see if he was there. I begged Gyömbi to let me sleep on the top bunk, but to no avail. She refused to swap with me, and I was stuck sleeping on the lower bunk.

I needed my mother more than ever, but we were not allowed to talk about her. Her existence was a big family secret. To those who did not know us, we all had same mother and father. It was as if Dad was ashamed of my mother. Not being able to talk about Mother or Valika caused me additional problems. I had difficulty sleeping and worse than that, I started to wet the bed. I became a bed wetter! I also started to suck my thumb. I hated what I was doing, but I could not help myself. I was called names and made fun of for the things I was doing. Often, I cried myself to sleep, and many nights I woke up screaming from nightmares.

Name calling actually started as soon as we became a blended family. My stepmother had a derogatory name for each child. Those names emphasized our own individual flaws. The names compounded our own insecurities and low self-esteem. After all, if our own parents found us defective and repulsive, how could others accept us?

My nickname was Csipás—crusty eyes. I had a blocked tear duct as a small child which caused my eyes to water and get crusty overnight. Although I cannot remember everyone's nickname, I do remember some. My oldest brother was called Csámpás due to the limp he had as a result of polio. Gyömbi was called Vaksa (blind) since she had little or no vision in one eye. Zsolt was called Pupos which means humpback and on and on went the name calling.

Overnight we went from being valued and loved to constantly being put down and ridiculed.

The new school year found us at a different school. With Dad's help we learned enough English over the summer to be able to do regular class work and be placed in our regular grades. Everyday he insisted we study English at home along with studying Hungarian. There was one hour of studying English and one hour of studying or at minimum reading Hungarian. Once a week we sang the Hungarian anthem and recited the Hungarian pledge. The family mantra was recited daily. It was, "Maradj mindig mindenhol Magyar." Loosely translated this means, "Always stay Hungarian everywhere." We were not allowed to speak English in the house only Hungarian since he feared we would forget our mother language. Conflict often arose as we studied various things in school which were a direct contradiction of what was taught in Hungary. This was especially true when we studied history.

Despite all of this, I liked my new school and I liked my class. I started making friends in school and it was great playing with other kids besides my siblings. We were not allowed to socialize with Americans outside of school, so I was never allowed to go to anyone's house to play after school, and no one was allowed to come to our house. Dad always said there were enough children in the house to play with already. He did not want us to assimilate. Other than school, the only other place we were allowed to go to was the Boys' Club for a few hours every evening. At the Boys' club we played ping pong, basketball, and cards. I loved to play cards the best. We not only had fun at the Club, but our English improved as well, and it kept us from getting in trouble which we managed to get into quite often.

I only saw my siblings during recess at our new school. When the bell rang, the entire school emptied, and all the students had recess together. Some played hopscotch while others played kickball. Tag was another game many of the children played, and we played cops and robbers. In the late 50's it was still okay to play those types of games! Often, I chose not to play, but instead I met up with my brothers at the side of the building. Across the street from where we met, was a convenience store. Students were not allowed to leave campus, but on any given day, there were students who did not follow those rules and left the campus to make various purchases at the store. Many times, we saw students have near misses as they dodged the cars as they crossed the busy street. On one winter day, a boy was trying to cross the street to return to school when the bell rang, and he was hit by a car. I, to this day, have a picture in my mind of the boy's bloody and mangled body. The rest of the school year was uneventful other than trying to adjust to the new culture we were living in especially since Dad fought our assimilation every step of the way.

The American customs were different. We had trouble understanding what we were allowed and not allowed to do but being around American children helped us learn what was acceptable behavior in the States. Since the two cultures were so different, problems arouse for us both at home and at school. Whenever we did something that my father did not like, we fought back with words such as, "Why did you bring us to America if you did not want us to be like Americans?" Whether it was from something as simple as the way we stated our names (in Hungary a person states last name first which is backwards from the way it is done in the US) to celebrating Halloween, problems arose. No, we were not allowed to go trick or treating. My father said, "I did not bring you to America to beg for candy! My children will not go out and beg!" As the years passed, Dad gave in, and we were allowed to go trick or treating. We never wore store bought costumes, but rather we made our own from things we had at home.

We did not celebrate Thanksgiving either. "That is an American holiday," Dad said. Instead, we celebrated St. Nicholas Day on December 6th. And for those of you who may not know that is the day Santa Claus brings candy to all good boys and girls. We kept the tradition for a few years after we came to the U.S., but in the later years, St. Nicholas Day was no longer celebrated in our house. I don't know why we stopped celebrating that holiday. Perhaps the reason may have been that we got older, or perhaps Dad just got tired of fooling with the whole thing. Our celebration of Christmas never changed though. Each year it was as if we stepped back in time, and we were back in Hungary. In our house, Christmas was always on December 24th. The angels brought the tree filled with candy on Christmas Eve, and we all received one present, an orange and some figs. As soon as it was dark outside, we marched into the living room, lined up from oldest to youngest and sang the Hungarian anthem as we entered the room. Between the 24th and the New Year, we were allowed to take candy off the tree. No, not at random, but each night we were allowed to choose one piece of candy until they were all gone.

Shortly after Christmas break, when I got home from school, I heard some chatter at our house about the Red Cross contacting my father. This was in January 1958 only a year after we arrived in the United States. As it turns out, my mother was frantically trying to locate me. On her way to work, on a bitter cold winter morning, her eyes caught a picture of me on the cover of a Hungarian magazine at a local news stand. She started to cry in a panic. "Where is Csilla? Where is my little girl?" In an attempt to find me, she contacted the Red Cross and asked for their help. They, in turn, located my father, and news was sent to her of my safety. I was in the

United States with the rest of the family, and I was well. Ironically, that picture was taken of me on one of our ski trips right before the revolution broke out. After things cooled down in Hungary, over a year after the photograph was taken, the photographer decided to use the picture as the cover of the January issue of Érdekes Ujság. Before I knew it, there were several copies of the magazine in our house. I was very proud.

The rest of the school year passed rather quickly, and the school year finally ended. Our summer vacation started with us being sent off to summer camp. I remember crying and being homesick. I don't believe I understood where I was going and what was happening. I felt I was taken from my home again. Although my family was dysfunctional, it was all I had. I was scared and when the counselors took my suitcase, I thought they were stealing my clothes. I tried to hold on, but they pried the suitcase out of my hands. Later that day when I got to my assigned cabin, I found my suitcase on my bed. I quickly opened it to see what was missing, but to my surprise, I found such items as shampoo, comb, brush, toothpaste, toothbrush, and even a couple of comic books neatly tucked amongst my clothes. I did not understand but was so grateful for their generosity! From that point on, I looked forward to summer camp each year, but that was the only year we went to camp.

As soon as we returned home, we were told we were moving to Ohio. Our lives were changing again. We were once more on the move.

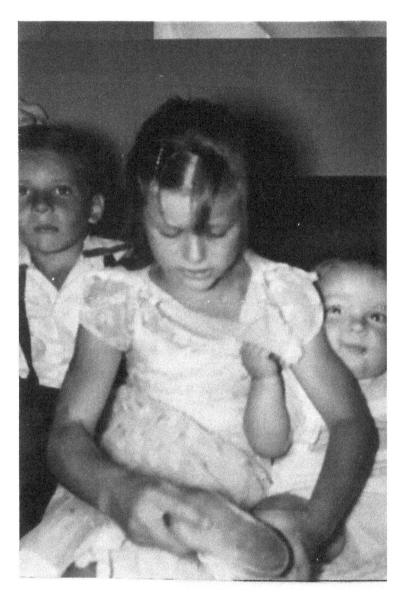

Taking care of a couple of my siblings

Chapter 6

Survival Mode

At age 9 we moved to Massillon, Ohio from Illinois. I was so happy to finally be away from Chicago. The memories of the two deaths I witnessed haunted me every night, and I was finally going to be able to sleep through the night without worrying about a dead man being under my bed!

The move to Massillon brought new challenges. We lived in a duplex with Anyu's five children on one side and my father, Mama and their children on the other side. I felt extremely alone and could not understand why we were being pushed away and punished that way. We had no one to take care of us. There was no adult supervision or guidance. We were on our own! The five of us took care of our side of the duplex. We washed, cleaned and fended for ourselves. The only time we were allowed on the other side of the house was to pick up our food and return our clean plates once we finished eating. Gyömbi became our surrogate mother.

There were difficulties in school as well. In 5th grade I found out I could not sing. I certainly sounded great to myself, so why did the teacher tell me I had to just move my mouth and pretend to sing the Christmas songs for the school program? She didn't want me to make a sound. She continued to say that it took ten people singing on key to offset my singing off key. I was humiliated. I wanted to just disappear! I received another blow that same day once I got home. Mama told me she heard a horrible sound coming from our side of the house, and it had to stop immediately or else. I did not confess I was the one making the noise. I was practicing tap dancing up and down the steps. I wanted to be the next Shirley Temple! I felt like I had been punched in the stomach for the second time that day. It wasn't fair. I loved to sing and dance, but now I was not allowed to do either. I was crushed!

On top of all that humiliation, my brothers and I decided to enter the school talent show at school. We were the Batizys, and we expected to take first place. We billed ourselves as the Batizy Gymnasts. When we didn't make it into the finals, we thought we were robbed, and we didn't mind telling everyone how we felt. In our own minds, we were the best. The judges just did not recognize talent when they saw it, or perhaps, they were prejudiced against foreigners. At any rate, we were crushed. Losing was never an option for us.

As young entrepreneurs we were always looking for opportunities to make a few dollars. One day we found an owl. We quickly decided to take him home and nurse him back to health since we convinced ourselves the bird was a rare species, and we could make millions of dollars once he got well. We did all we could to help the poor bird, but to no avail. The bird died in a few days and our dreams and hopes of becoming millionaires were dashed.

After school we always played outside until dark. One afternoon while playing outside, I stepped on a board with the nail sticking out of it. I screamed and cried from the pain, and no matter how hard I tried to remove the nail and the board, I was not able to do it. I wanted to take care of it myself because I did not want to get in trouble for being careless. Although I begged my brothers not to tell, one of them ran inside and out came Dad. Father managed to remove the board and took me inside. He cleaned out the wound and had me soak my foot, but it got infected anyway, and I was out of school for several days. When I was finally able to go back to school, I was sporting a brand-new pair of shoes. Prior to that, most clothing items, including shoes, were hand me downs. The bottom of the shoes often had holes in them. So, for that reason, getting injured and almost losing my foot was worth it to me. I finally got a new pair of shoes!

When we first arrived in Massillon the family activities consisted of playing soccer in the park and going hiking. Since I was a girl, I was always one of the goalies. The other goalie was my sister Gyömbi. I did not want to play soccer, but the choice was not mine. The hikes the family took weren't fun either. We left early in the morning and did not get home until late at night. Our lunch consisted of two slices of day-old bread and a thick slice of cheese placed between those slices. We never took water with us, and after hiking for hours, we were tired and thirsty. The last thing we wanted was to eat the dry bread, but we forced every bite down without too much protest. Some of us deliberately fell behind the pack just so we could sneak water from the hose attached to houses we passed. We risked getting caught by Father just to be able to get a sip or two of water. For us, it was a matter of survival. What could have been a fun outing always turned into something to be dreaded, and something we hated with a passion.

One day those activities were replaced by swimming. We did a little swimming in Chicago, but now we were taking it to the next level. My father decided competitive swimming is what we were going to do. His children were going to the Olympics. Dad coached us, and our practices were grueling. Once we started swimming there was no time for anything else. Everybody swam whether they wanted to or not. We were, after all, "The Swimming Batizys." We had school, homework, chores and swimming. I didn't mind. I actually enjoyed the structure, and I was an excellent swimmer.

Our next move took us to Columbus. We lived at 646 Wilson Avenue in Columbus, Ohio. We stayed there for 3 years while Father did his residency. The family was in for some major changes once more. The size of the family grew. We grew from 11 children to 13, we no longer lived in a duplex, and the family joined a swim club. Up until then, the family swam and even attended a few swim-meets. Swimming was just another family activity we did during the summer. Little did I know, once we joined the swim team, we would be swimming year-round. At first it was fun, and we enjoyed the recognition we received as the Swimming Batizys. We attended swim meets, and wherever we went the media was there. They'd line us up from tallest to shortest and take our picture. The next morning, we eagerly waited for the paper to see our picture and the accompanying story. The story was always the same of how Doctor Batizy and his wife escaped Hungary with their eleven children. The story had to be fascinating to others, or why else would reporters take their time to cover it? To me, the reporters missed the story. The story should have been about how we got to the swim meets with all fifteen (by this time two more children were born) of us piled into the family car which was not a station wagon but a four-door sedan. We were packed in like a bunch of sardines. We were literally on top of each other.

In time we started attending two day meets that were quite a distance from our home and we had to spend the night. Spending the night in a hotel room might have been a treat for some people, but for the Swimming Batizys it was a circus. We all slept in one room. The top mattresses were removed, and before you knew it, we had four beds. I hated spending the night away from home. There were too many people in such a small space! By this time the family grew to ten boys and three girls. The youngest child was my baby sister, Hajna, who is 11 years younger than me. She was an infant, and she slept in one of the drawers that was converted into a baby bed. As you can imagine, the sleeping arrangement was a nightmare and so was trying to use one bathroom with all those people.

We traveled in our swimsuits and did not take change of clothes when we first started swimming. In fact, we traveled in our suits and stayed in our suits the whole time. What a sight we must have been! I imagined people thought we were a bunch of gypsies. It was extremely embarrassing to me, though I did not show my embarrassment. As you recall, it was not acceptable to show emotions in our family, so I never voiced my opinion on how ridiculous I thought we looked. I wasn't about to create waves! The price I would have paid for those thoughts would have been too painful physically! I didn't need a backhand to my face for opening my mouth. It simply wasn't worth it. I, however, was glad to see cold weather arrive. During the winter months we, at least, had warm-up suits to cover our bathing suits. My stepmother got us gray sweatshirts and sweatpants, and Gyömbi and I wrote Batizy on the back of the shirts underlined in red, white and green which are the colors of the Hungarian flag, and our number was stenciled on the right sleeve. I was number six. I was the sixth oldest from the top in the blended family.

I don't know what my brothers and sisters thought about how we were living, but I found it appalling. I felt embarrassed and ashamed about how we looked, what we did, and how I thought others perceived us. I just wanted to hide and distance myself from the circus like atmosphere our family created. The older I got the stronger this feeling of wanting to hide from the family became. I did not belong, and I knew I had to get away. Survival mode became my only friend. I was emotionally detached!

When school started, I was in 6th grade and attended Main Street Elementary School. We rode our bikes to and from school most days. Yes, we upgraded from roller skates to bicycles shortly after we arrived in Columbus. We shoveled snow in the cold winters and saved our money to buy those bikes. No, they were not new, but we were proud to have them just the same. We purchased the bicycles from one of the police auctions.

Heading home from school, Botond and I often rode our bikes in back alleys. It was a shortcut to our house. Often, we enjoyed picking apples off the apple tree we encountered in our travel home. Now, don't get me wrong, we did not go on anyone's property. As fate would have it, one of the branches hung into the ally which, of course, made the apples fair game. Those apples were so crunchy and juicy. They were delicious. We actually talked to Mama about the branch and the apples, and she told us we could pick those apples. Well, the man who lived in the house whose property the apple tree was on did not share our opinion, and he got angrier and angrier each and every day. Finally, he had enough and was waiting for us to come by his house. As Botond and I approached the hanging branch, we got off our bikes and started to pick some apples. Out of nowhere the man came at us. I told Botond in Magyar—the language spoken in Hungary, "On the count of three, we will jump on our bicycles and ride away." As planned, I counted to three and jumped on my bike and rode as fast as I could. Botond froze and the man grabbed his bike and came after me. I maneuvered the bike in and out of allies until I got home. When the man got to my house and told Mama I stole his apples, I was in big trouble. I was punished in front of the man and then punished again when I protested. I didn't understand what was happening since we were told we could pick the apples. When I close my eyes, I can still feel the sting of the slap across my face, not because of the pain, but because of the unfairness of it all.

In the early 60s there was no such thing as the women's movement. I was way ahead of my time as far as equality for women was concerned. Females were treated as less than. The winters were extremely cold in Ohio, so, one day, I decided to wear pants to school. I was cold! After a few days I was called into the principal's office and was given a letter to take home stating I was not to attend school in pants. I thought of the unfairness of this policy and protested to anyone who I thought could help my cause, but to no avail. It was dresses or be sent home from school. Once more my voice was silenced. Yes, I complied and wore a dress every day to school from that day forward.

At the end of the school year, my 6th grade class had a graduation program. I got a new dress from Sears for the occasion. A brand-new dress was something I was not accustomed to, so I was extra grateful to receive it. I had a new dress, and I wanted to look extra nice for the program. Many of the girls in my class already started shaving their legs and under arms. I was not one of those girls. In Hungary, females did not shave. My stepmother did not shave, my sister Gyömbi did not shave, but I decided it was time for me to start, so I did. I got my father's razor and carefully shaved my legs and under arms. Of course, I ended up with cuts on my legs, but I was proud of the bold step I took. I did not think of the consequences of my actions for disgracing the family. I was told that I was no better than a common street walker since only street walkers shaved their legs! I hated America and wanted to be back home. It was obvious the two cultures were very different. Why did Dad bring us to this country if we were not allowed to follow what was acceptable here? I just did not understand. Obviously, assimilation was not in his vocabulary.

Besides the difficulties of adjusting to living in America, growing up in a predominately male house was also a challenge. In our home in America it was always about the boys which was opposite of the way it was in Hungary. Back in Budapest, Valika always treated the girls special. We were valued as human beings. Here in the States, the girls, except for my sister Hajna who was still very young, were in the home to serve the boys. We had no value since we were unlikely to carry the Batizy name forward. Our roll in the house was to clean, wash, iron, vacuum, babysit the younger siblings, and do whatever was considered as a female job. Mama told us that we had to learn how to keep house because that was what we were going to do once we married. She was preparing us for adulthood! In reality we were her maids. She checked the beds after we made them, and often, she would pull the bedding off because she didn't like how we made the beds. The boys had it made. I thought it was unfair that they got to do fun things while Gyömbi and I tended to the house. I often thought to myself that I would show her and the rest of the clan that I, Csilla, was going to be more than just a housewife. I was going to be a teacher.

I was not prepared for puberty. When I started developing and refused to wear just swim trunks to the pool a major uproar developed, and a family fight ensued. I needed a bathing suit not trunks. The need for feminine products, a bra and other things that a growing girl needed was the next challenge. Everything was a battle to get. Although Gyömbi was older than me, she offered little or no help. She was an early bloomer and those things were provided to her from the beginning. I, on the other hand, being a late developer and a huge tomboy, had to beg for all the necessities.

I hated everything that was happening and wished for those wonderful years in Hungary. Valika would have made sure I had everything I needed and more!

During those special times of the month when I could not go swimming, I was ridiculed. I can still hear my brothers saying, "Why is Csilla not swimming? It isn't fair she gets to skip practice." "Why," I asked myself, "was it an issue?" It was never an issue about Gyömbi not swimming, but it was always an issue for me not to swim. Sometimes, I just wanted to cry, but I reminded myself tears were not allowed. Tears were a sign of weakness, and I was not weak! I could do anything my brothers did. I quickly learned to suck it up, and not let them know they got under my skin.

I believe the three years the family lived in Columbus were the hardest years of my life. There were many family fights with mother's children taking a stand against what we perceived as unfair treatment we received. I remember one particular Christmas when Zsolt and Botond had to take Christmas presents to school for their Christmas party. Botond was given a very nice gift to exchange with a student plus a nice gift for his teacher. Zsolt was sent to school with a bundle of funeral home calendars my stepmother took out of a dumpster to exchange with one of his classmates. The student who received the calendars got upset and cried. The teacher luckily had an extra gift to give the boy, but in order to make things right, she announced to the class that those funeral calendars were the only thing Zsolt could afford. This humiliated him. As if that wasn't enough, she went on to tell her students that Christmas was about giving, and since Zsolt was poor, they each needed to give him something. One by one the boys and girls gave Zsolt their gifts. The more things he received the worse Zsolt felt!

That same Christmas several of us received a transistor radio for Christmas. We got a cheap, used am radio while Botond got a nice, new and expensive am/fm radio. When we voiced our dissatisfaction, Mama simply informed us that since we were tone deaf, we did not need anything better than what we got. This led to yet another family argument. The way we were treated as compared to the others was just plain wrong, and we were never too shy to point out the obvious. Often, after those family feuds, we slept in the detached garage as we were locked out of the house. We'd huddle together trying to keep warm and prayed for our safety. To make things worse, those fights were not only verbal but also physical. Dad had little or no control over the situations, and when he came home from work and found himself in the middle of one of those fights, we knew where his allegiance was. He always sided with Mama and the second family. This only made things worse for us and made us feel extremely alone.

There was so much turmoil going on in our lives, and to top it off, we nearly lost my brother Zsolt. One day, as he was riding his bicycle, he was hit by a car. This happened on a busy highway on his way home from swim practice. I can't even imagine how he survived that ordeal. Later that day as he was fixing his bicycle, his hand got caught in the gears. I can still hear him screaming in pain and can visualize my father pulling his hand out of the chain. Once Dad saw he was going to be okay, he was punished for being careless. By being punished, I mean physically beaten. We always got punished for being careless when an accident happened, and as usual, the older siblings got punished as well for not taking care of the younger ones. Being a year older than Zsolt, I got punished too.

An 8th grade requirement for girls was to take home economics and for the boys to take shop. I did not want to take home economics. I wanted to take shop. I loved making things with my hands. I was good at it! The first semester I was in cooking class, and the second semester I took sewing. I did not mind the sewing part, but cooking was another thing. My cooking class teacher did not like me. She was extremely mean and always blamed me for things I didn't do. Furthermore, she never bothered to learn my name, and when I did not respond to the wrong name, she yelled at me. She mispronounced my name to the point that one day I could not take it any longer and spoke up, and she chased me around the class-room kitchen table. Round and round we went until one of the other kids grabbed me and held me down. When the teacher caught up with me, she slapped me across my face and to top it off at the end of the semester she gave me a D! That really stung. I was scared to take the D home, but to my surprise, I did not get in trouble.

One day while I was walking back to school from lunch, a man jumped out of the bushes and grabbed me. As I was screaming and fighting back, I saw two of my brothers turning the corner and I yelled to them for help. The man quickly took off running and disappeared. Later that evening Gyömbi noticed someone peeping through our bedroom window. We were terrified! My sister and I started dressing and undressing in our bedroom closet in hopes that no one would see us while we were changing clothes.

Shortly after that incident we saw someone in our bedroom late one night. We screamed, but before we could even turn the lights on, the person was gone. We started to sleep with our windows shut and locked even though there was no air conditioning in the house and our room was extremely hot and stuffy. For added protection, we wrapped our blankets tightly around us so that if someone came in, we would wake up if that person tried to touch or molest us. We lived in constant fear! This is how life was in Columbus, but near the end of eighth grade, we were told we were moving. The news could not have come at a better time.

1960-1962 Columbus, Ohio

We became the "Swimming Batizys"

Chapter 7

Teen Years

I had high hopes for my life in Nashville. After all, it was a new beginning. I was excited about the move. Little did I know Nashville would present new challenges and drastic changes to the family. I was not prepared for those changes.

Dad got a job as one of the psychiatrists at Central State Mental Hospital and we lived on the grounds. A row of beautiful houses was provided for several of the doctors and their families. This was different from any other living arrangements we had before. The grounds were beautiful, and the patients mowed our lawn and did our laundry which meant we had fewer chores to do. Life was really looking up.

There were some difficulties facing us in Nashville, however. Up north we always lived in Hungarian communities. Everything was within walking distance. In Nashville everything was spread out, and the only way to get around was by car. So, it was in Nashville that we were introduced to hitchhiking. That is how we got around. My survival instinct and God's love kept me safe. This was true for my brother Zsolt as well. One day, while he was hitchhiking home from swim practice, he was almost abducted. His instinct kicked in, though, and he jumped out of the moving car. It was a miracle he survived since the near abduction happened on an extremely busy highway.

On the upside, we no more got to Nashville when we started swimming for our new swim team. We swam for Swim 'n Sun Cabana Club. I liked everything about my new team including the girls who I competed against. I was probably the second-best swimmer in the 13-14 years old age group. No matter how hard I tried, I could never beat my teammate, Rita. It did not take long for me to realize if I wanted a gold medal, I would have to enter events she was not swimming in; otherwise, I would end up with an inevitable second place. Like I said, no matter how hard I practiced, Rita always beat me. I guess she was a better swimmer, and maybe even a more talented swimmer than me.

I loved being part of that swim team. I felt a certain sense of belonging that I always longed for and had not felt since my arrival to the United States. I remember on my 14th birthday the team members gave me a surprise birthday party. I got some very nice clothes and various other things. My team was like a family to me.

By the following summer I was no longer permitted to swim. The sense of belonging was once more taken from me. Instead of swimming, I was tasked with babysitting my younger siblings and doing housework. When I asked why I was not allowed to swim, I got hit and was told swimming for girls was a waste of money. We couldn't afford it. It's strange how those same words or similar words were echoed years later by my husband when I wanted to return to college.

As with everything else in the past, all emphasis was now on the boys. It was always about the boys. After all, boys could get swimming scholarships to attend college which was not available to girls in the 60s. And, if I may add, they did. One by one my brothers went off to college on swimming scholarships. Dad's dreams and hopes of one of his children becoming an Olympic swimmer was gone, but swimming still provided a means of getting into a good college for the boys, so the swimming continued for them.

My sister Gyömbi started college that fall, and I was the only girl left in the house besides my baby sister. Csaba and Gábor left the house too. They took off for California. The family was changing! One by one the older children were leaving. I wanted to go too! I told myself to hang in there. As soon as I graduate from high school I, too, will leave. I, like my older brothers and sister, felt we were being pushed out of the house one by one, and so I was biding my time to have my turn to leave.

Once someone left, they were gone. I suspect I've seen my brother, Csaba, perhaps 3-4 times since he left the house in 1963. He ended up living most of his life in New Mexico. He and his wife made their home in Albuquerque. His death in October 2009 did not come as a shock to any of us since he had been sick for many years prior to his death. In fact, the doctors never expected him to live as long as he did. He had several close calls before but managed to cheat death each time to the amazement of his doctors.

Many of my siblings spoke at his funeral sharing stories of various adventures they had with Csaba. There were stories of him saving our brother Szabolcs's life. Did that really happen? I had no recollection of that. I did not remember any of the things my brothers and sister shared. How could that be? Did I grow up in the same house? No, I did not get up to speak. I had nothing to say since I did not know my brother. He was a stranger to me. The truth is, I had become so accustomed to avoiding conflict, I became emotionally detached from the family. I was in survival mode.

It wasn't until school started that the stigma of living at Central State became an issue. I often heard laughter and jokes about where we lived. And if it wasn't jokes about living at Central State, it was about being a Yankee. The fact is, being a Yankee while living in the South caused major issues.

Wasn't it enough that I learned English? Now the English I learned was ridiculed. I was just fine with saying "you guys" instead of "you all", or "over there" instead of "over yonder," but I had to adapt or endure teasing. I chose to adapt since being a teenager was hard enough without being made fun of and bullied. I wanted to fit in. I wanted to be accepted.

I did not go to 9th grade. I went straight from 8th grade to becoming a sophomore. In Columbus, Ohio you could take high school courses if you excelled in academics. I managed to earn a couple of high school credits while in 8th grade, and I attended summer school once we arrived in Nashville. For that reason, when school started, I was placed in tenth grade. Antioch High School was very different from Roosevelt Jr. High. I did not look or dress the same as the girls in my class. They wore makeup and their hair was teased, and they looked all grown up. I did not fit in, but before long I started rolling my hair and I learned to tease and comb my hair like the other girls. I saved my lunch money and bought lipstick, hairspray and any other items I felt I needed to fit in with my peers. I joined the marching band that same year. Okay, I already knew I had no musical talent, but that did not stop my desire to be a band member. Being tone deaf was a slight handicap in my eyes but not a show-stopper. Not only did I join the band, but I talked one of my younger siblings into joining as well. I knew I would have no opposition from Mama once Botond said that he wanted to be in the band too, and sure enough before long I was playing the clarinet in Antioch High School's marching band.

The band opened up some great economic opportunities for us, none of which had anything to do with music. It wasn't long before we found a way to make some money. During the fall fundraiser we made a huge profit from selling candy bars. It did not take us long to find the perfect scheme. By going out of our school zone to sell the candy bars we could double the price and make a 100% profit off each bar. I am not sure where our entrepreneurial spirit came from, but whenever an opportunity presented itself, we were ready to take advantage of it. And did we ever!

Summer 1964

Teen years in Nashville

Chapter 8

Reconnecting With Valika

I t was during my sophomore year that my grandmother Valika came to live with us. I had not seen her since December 1956 and now here she was. My sister Gyömbi no longer lived at home. She married in December, her freshman year in college, so Valika and I shared a bedroom. I loved her being here in the United States, though the adjustment was very hard for her. She had no trouble telling her son of any unfair treatment or unequal treatment of the children. It was so nice to have an adult in my corner for a change. You know, an advocate for my well being. I was grateful for that. Finally, I felt loved again.

As time passed, I was not just her granddaughter, but had become her best friend and confidant. We talked for hours, and I did things with and for her. When Dad refused to take her to the salon to get her hair fixed as she was accustomed to in Hungary, I fixed her hair for her. It did not matter if she needed a cut, perm or just wanted me to comb her hair, I was there. I finally had my Valika back. I felt safe, happy and special once more.

By my junior year I was ready to date. Can you imagine my excitement when one day someone asked me out for a date? That excitement soon dissipated when I realized Dad would never let me go. I didn't know how I was going to get my father to allow me to go out. No one in the family had ever asked about going out on a date while in high school. Oh no, once more I was the first one to go against family tradition. Of course, I couldn't let this minor problem keep me from accepting the date. I would just have to wait for the right moment to break the news to my father. At first, he said no, but after crying, pleading and arguing, he finally caved and told me I could go. I could not believe my good fortune. I was actually going on a date!

I was very nervous when date night rolled around, but at the same time I felt triumphant. I was going on a date while still in high school. My joy, however, quickly turned to embarrassment when my father told me that my grandmother was going as a chaperone. Some things never change. It was always like this with Father. It was a tug-of-war between two cultures. No, this cannot be! Here it was a few hours before my date and now I had to deal with this. I told him this was unheard of in the United States, but it was either taking her or not going. He won.

When my date came to the door to pick me up and realized what was about to happen, he didn't appear happy. Who could blame him? But at least the date was still on, and we went to the movies as planned. After the movie we ate at Shoney's then home. I don't recall going on another date while in high school. It wasn't because I didn't want to go. I would have loved going out again, but no one asked me. I am sure the whole school heard through the grapevine about my grandmother chaperoning the date. I am sure I was the laughingstock of my class. I was crushed. I blamed my grandmother for my lack of social life, because she went with me, but I knew deep inside it was not her choice either. I did not stay angry with her for long.

In the fall of 1963, my brother Levente went off to school to the University of Alabama. I was now the oldest child at home. That did not last long though since my sister Tünde was finally allowed to come to the United States. After all these years, my sister and I were being reunited. I had not seen her for 6 years. By now, I was 15 and she was 21. I had so much to teach her about life in the United States. The first of which was for me to tell her she had to shave. I told her it was not acceptable for her to go around with body hair. At first, she protested but once I explained to her that she looked like a hairy bear, she gave in, and I helped her with her first shave. We did many things together the next two years. Even after she married her sweetheart, I was included in various activities and outings. It was as if the years had rolled back.

A couple of months before my high school graduation the family moved to Illinois. Usually the moves occurred right after school was out for the summer, but this time the move was during the school year. Arrangements were made for me to stay with one of Dad's colleagues, Dr. Siegmann and his family. Living with the Siegmanns was wonderful. I was treated just like one of their own. I even got a weekly allowance. This was the first time in my life I got money for no reason at all. I felt as if I had died and gone to heaven. I really liked being there!

The day before graduation, I got word of Valika's death. I had seen her just a few months prior when I took the Greyhound bus to Downey, IL for a visit. It was during Easter break. While I was there, we talked about many things. She told me how unhappy she was living in the United States. She talked about wanting to go back to Hungary, but Dad would not allow her to leave. She hated living in America. I promised her I would be back during the summer and things would be different, but she couldn't hold on that long. The next time I saw her was at the funeral, and once more my only connection to my home as a happy child was gone. I felt as if my world caved in on me once more.

Spending time with Valika

Chapter 9

Enough Is Enough

Downey, Illinois was never my home. I stayed there after Valika's funeral for a few weeks, but I could not adjust. I was angry about Valika's death and did not want to be near or around the family. During those weeks I had several altercations with my father. One day when he hit me, I mustered up the courage to hit him back. I simply had enough.

The following night I decided to run away and made plans to leave when the family was asleep. I pinned my long hair up, placed a baseball cap on top of my head and for an added touch, I dressed in my brother Zsolt's clothes. I figured, if I looked like a boy, I would be safe as I was making my way to Tennessee. I heard many stories about murders and other horrible things happening to people who were hitchhiking, and I did not intend to be yet another statistic. Once my mind was made up, there was no stopping me, and the next thing I knew I was lowering myself out of the second story bedroom window in the middle of the night. I was on my way to Nashville to be with Tűnde and her husband, Robert.

It seemed as if my journey had just begun when it came to an abrupt end. Several cars stopped as I was making my way toward the interstate to offer me a ride, but I managed to ignore them all until a car stopped and the people in the car convinced me to go home with them. A quick survey of the people in the car led me to make the decision to take them up on their offer. I felt I would be safe with them. Instead of Nashville, I ended up only a couple of streets from my parents' house. I stayed there for a few weeks before I got a nagging feeling I needed to leave, and that is exactly what I did. When I returned home, nothing was said, and no questions were asked. Instead, Dad got me a ticket on the Greyhound and put me on the bus. I was heading to Nashville. That was the last time I lived with my family. In fact, I did not see nor talk with my father for years after that except one time. I was 16 and on my own. Well, not quite on my own, since I stayed with my sister, Tünde, until school started.

My sister Gyömbi's in-laws took me in once school started. They lived in Murfreesboro, TN. I took out a student loan and entered college. I liked college and enjoyed the freedom I was given by Sibyl and Pete. I was allowed to come and go as I pleased, but I never took advantage of the situation. I even had the privilege of using their car to get me to my classes. Living there was very pleasant. I think I would have stayed there forever, but life happens, and things change. As fate would have it, Pete was diagnosed with cancer and it became evident I needed to leave.

I met my husband the first day of classes, and we started dating soon thereafter. When he lost his student deferment and was drafted into the army, he proposed, and I accepted. That was in 1966.

Since I was under-age, I had to have parental permission to marry. I reached out to my father, but he refused to sign the paper. He was furious! I did not understand why he was angry since I no longer lived in his house. He was not supporting me, so why did he refuse to give his permission for me to marry? It did not make any sense at all. That's okay, I thought, Mother will sign for me, and I will show Dad he can no longer control me. And so it was, I wrote my mother in Budapest and she gave her written permission.

Summer 1965 after I ran away from home

Chapter 10

Mother

In 1968 I was reunited with my mother for the first time since 1956. My brothers, sisters and I pooled our money together and brought her to the States for a visit. It was so good to see her. The years melted away, and it was as if we had just seen and talked with her yesterday. From that point on, Mother came to the United States every other year. I finally become somebody's Csilike (Hungarian term of endearment) once more. And that is how it was and how it remained until she died in January 2000.

The trip to my homeland for my mother's funeral was emotional. Thankfully my son, Blake, made the trip with me and gave me the support I needed. By the time our plane landed in Budapest, I was a total wreck. We made our way out of the airport and hailed a taxi to take us to our hotel. I got visibly frustrated with our driver. I kept giving him directions to where we were going, and he just looked at me as if I was speaking in a foreign language. My son finally leaned over to me and said, "Mom, why don't you give him directions in Hungarian? You speak the language fluently."

Prior to her death, every time I saw Anyu or talked with her on the telephone she asked me to come to Budapest to visit her. Each time she asked me, I made a promise to her I would come. Perhaps next year, or the year after that was my standard answer when she tried to pin me down for a date. I think we both knew I would never make the trip over there, but the invite was always there none-the-less. It was for that reason the trip back home at the time of her death was so difficult for me. I was guilt ridden with the knowledge that it took her death to finally get me there. I felt selfish and self-centered. After all, I put everything and everybody ahead of her and never made the trip back home while she was alive. Even as I write this, I have tears in my eyes. She asked so little of me and I was not willing to grant her that request. Sure, money was tight, but I always managed to find the money for everything else. At that moment, after all the years of pent up emotions, mental pain, and stress, I realized I even shunned the one person I wanted to stay with the most. I was a mess! I remember being in her apartment and breaking down and crying as I looked around and saw her humble surroundings. I whispered, "Anyuka, I am here."

When I left Hungary after her funeral, I knew in my heart I would never go back there again. The pain was too great. Both my children visited my birthplace several times and plan on going back as often as they can. For me it was different. Although I have pride in my heritage, I still struggled with my past, so for that reason, I chose to stay away, at least for now.

Years later I did return. I spent a wonderful week in Budapest and visited my childhood home, the school I attended, and where my mother worked. I even ice skated with my daughter at the rink where I learned to skate so many years ago. The journey back home brought closure for me. During the week we were there I cried for the little girl who was torn from her life in Hungary, but I also laughed and smiled at the memories of my early childhood living in a loving home being cared for by my mother and my grandmother Valika. It was truly a wonderful trip!

Mother in 1968 and Mother and Lenti in 1981

Some of Anyu's many trips to the States

Szent János Korház where Mother worked, and I went to kindergarten

59 years later, dinner cruise on the Danube River on Christmas Eve Jeff, Lenti, Csilla, Lou

Chapter 11
Adulthood And Finding Myself

My childhood experiences spilled into my adult life. I had two marriages. I entered into each one with hopes of finding the happiness I could only dream of and the person I could live happily ever after with. I thought, by working hard, I could and would earn the love and respect I was searching for all my life. After all, I learned in my formative years that I could find peace and perhaps earn a new dress by going above and beyond what was expected. As it turned out, my efforts only led to resentment and making me feel more worthless and unloved.

At first glance, you'd think the two men were polar opposites. My first husband was quiet, reserved, penny-wise and controlling. My second husband was outgoing, life of the party, money flowed through his fingers like there was no tomorrow and didn't care what I did or didn't do as long as I was a good provider. There was, however, one thing both men had in common. It was their love for their child (children). This was evidenced by their involvement in their activities.

My first marriage lasted a little over 13 years, and my second marriage lasted nearly 21 years. In all honesty, there were some good times in both marriages, but those were often overshadowed by the challenges that life brought. What I was looking for in my marriages was a partner, a teammate, but I did not find that in either marriage.

As I stated earlier, I married my first husband in April 1966. He had been drafted into the army after losing his student deferment and since those times were so unpredictable with the Vietman War, when he asked me to marry him, I said, "Yes." Within a few short weeks after our marriage he left for service.

He did his basic training at Fort Benning, GA, and at the completion of basic training he was transferred to Ft. Gordon, GA where he became a military policeman. It was at this point I was allowed to join him.

Shortly after we arrived at Ft. Gordon, we rented a studio apartment in Augusta, GA. I loved my new home at first, but it wasn't long after we moved in, I heard sounds coming from the outside. When I investigated, I realized there was someone outside peeping through the window. Thoughts of Columbus, Ohio returned, and I was more scared and terrified than ever. My husband worked the night shift on post, so I was all alone each and every night. To protect myself, I grabbed the shotgun we owned and sat in the middle of the bed until the "peeping Tom" left. This became a nightly ritual for me for the next two years. I lived in constant fear for my safety, but I was not going out without a fight.

To help make ends meet, I worked at K-Mart Foods as a cashier. I left that job because of sexual advances being made by one of my coworkers. That was the first of many times I had to deal with that type of behavior at the workplace. For the most part, I was able to fight off the sexual advances, but there were a couple of times I couldn't get away. Some men in authority felt they could do whatever they wanted to female employees. That was how things were back in those days. After leaving my job at K-Mart Foods, I worked at the Post Exchange on the military base in the shoe department.

After my husband received his honorable discharge from the army, we headed back to Tennessee where I was able to secure a job as a dental assistant while he returned to school to pursue a degree. I was happy to do whatever it took to help him get through school which included tutoring him and helping him with his homework assignments. I was happy to help. I was investing in our future.

About five years into the marriage we decided it was time to start a family. After what seemed like an eternity, it was obvious we could not get pregnant. We sought medical help and were told pregnancy was impossible. Although the news was devastating, my desire to have a baby did not end. With my upcoming birthday, I told him that my birthday wish was for us to apply to the state for adoption. And that is exactly what we did. Once all the forms were filled out, and home visits completed, we were approved. This was such a high point in our lives. We were going to be parents in the future. The timeline given to us was 2-3 years.

Seven short months later, on March 1, 1972 I received a telephone call at work from the state that our son was born on February 29, 1972 and he would be coming home on March 3rd. We had two days to get ready for his arrival. I am, to this day, so grateful to my friends for helping us get the nursery together. My dear friend Elaine and others were there to teach me how to make formula, and to help me with everything else to ensure we were ready.

Early morning on the 3ʳᵈ there was a knock on the front door. With great joy and excitement, I opened the door to find our case worker standing there with a tiny baby boy in her arms. As she handed me my son, I asked her if she had any instructions. She replied, "Just love him!" We named our son Blake. He is our gift from God.

I was a stay-at-home mom for a year which was a state requirement. Even though our son was in our home from the time he left the hospital, the birth mother had legal rights to change her mind about the adoption for a full year. As you can imagine, I stayed stressed the whole year until the adoption process was completed.

At the end of the year, I was permitted to return to work, but I had no intention of doing that. I saw myself as a stay-at-home mom, but that didn't materialize. As soon as the year was up, my husband pressured me to return to work and as a good, obedient wife, I returned to my old job as a dental assistant.

It did not take long for me to realize I needed to go back to school and get my degree to be able to get a decent paying job to offset day care costs and other expenses. My childhood dream of becoming a teacher resurfaced and my desire to return to school became an obsession, but every time I brought up the subject, I was told we couldn't afford it.

What? We can't afford for me to return to school. This was not acceptable to me. I was both shocked and hurt by his response. I took a stand and finally spoke what was on my mind. "When is it my turn? I worked to put you through school, but you are denying me the same opportunity. This is not fair, and I refuse to accept what you think we can or cannot afford."

It took some time, but my determination to follow what I believed was best for the family led me to work during the day and attend school at night. I left my dental assistant job and started working for an insurance company which had better hours and weekends off. This allowed me to enroll in school. In 1975 I received my B.S. degree in education with high honors. My childhood dream, as a result of my hard work, came true, but not without a cost.

Working days and going to school at night took its toll on our marriage. In retrospect, I believe his insecurities kicked into overdrive. Almost daily I heard him say, "When you get your degree, you will leave me." I didn't understand why he was saying those words, and why he was pushing me away. At one point I suggested counseling but was ridiculed for the suggestion. After all, according to him, I was the one who changed, not him.

He was right. I did change. I was no longer that 17-year-old child he married. Over the years I had grown up and realized that marriage was both give and take. I got tired of always giving but never receiving. I was tired. Nothing I did was ever good enough. I started having flashbacks of my childhood growing up in America, so in 1978 the marriage ended in divorce.

In December 1979 on Christmas Eve, I met my second husband at a Christmas party which, by the way, I had no desire to attend. After a whirlwind romance, we married in June 1980, but not before he finished college. Seriously, who drops out of school when they are one quarter from graduating? That, to me, was unbelievable especially since he often talked about some financial issues he was having at the time. By getting his degree, he was able to multiple his income substantially.

Although things appeared great from the outside, there were serious issues from the start. In fact, as my brother started walking me down the aisle, I told him, "I think I am making a mistake." He quickly replied, "It's too late," and he proceeded to walk me down the aisle. I smiled, and I just passed those feelings off as normal wedding jitters. Surely, all brides have those same feelings, I told myself.

Soon after we married, he wanted us to start our own family. I was okay with that for the most part, but I did have some concerns. Between the two of us, we already had three children, and with his spending habits, could we even afford a fourth child? How will the older children feel about a baby brother or sister coming into their lives? I knew how my son felt. For years he had asked for a baby brother or baby sister. I knew he would be thrilled. As for my stepdaughters, I had no clue. On October 23, 1981, little over a year later, our daughter, Lenti, was born. I received my second gift from God.

I was the primary breadwinner in the family. Throughout the nearly 21 years of marriage, I worked a minimum of two jobs to supplement my teacher's salary. No job was beneath me. I sold Tupperware, tutored at night, assembled boxes in our garage for a corrugated box company, sold dolls that I handmade from socks, and hand-painted special-order sweatshirts for friends and co-workers. I worked hard to make sure we did not lose our house, and to make sure we had food, water, and electricity.

I was, not only, the financial provider, but I was the responsible adult in the home establishing structure and rules for all the children. For him, it was all about fun and games, especially, when the older children came for the weekend. The house rules did not seem to apply to them which triggered painful memories of my own upbringing in a dysfunctional blended family. I had to protect my children. When I spoke up about this inequality I was immediately ridiculed and was referred to as a "Debbie Downer." To me, the house rules had to be applied equally, and since this was not the case, I seriously considered ending the marriage numerous times, but hung in there for my daughter's sake.

Yes, he was working and making good money, but his income was rarely applied toward our household needs. The money he earned was spent on his hobbies, which included country club membership, golf, Nascar races, and football games which he usually attended with his buddies. Occasionally, however, there were activities that included the children. There were some road trips to both Ohio and Alabama to visit my family and, of course, going to Opryland for a family outing. Those trips, however, were few and far between. While he played, I worked to make sure there was money for the necessities of life. Once again, I was taking care of everybody else, but didn't take time to take care of myself. What I didn't know at that time was that by shouldering all the financial and other respon-sibilities, I was enabling him. I had become an enabler of all the things I hated and wanted gone from the marriage.

A chance encounter with a psychologist changed my life. I was not seeking professional help, but out of the blue this person asked me a question which led me to seek counseling. You might be won-dering what that question was. He simply asked me if I read a cer-tain book. Before the day ended, I, not only purchased the book, but also started reading it. As I got deeper and deeper into the book, I realized I needed help. After two years of therapy, I was able to deal with the childhood traumas I lived through and other issues that came my way throughout my adult life.

In one of the early sessions my therapist asked, "Why are you still in survival mode? What are you trying to survive?" My answer to him was a child's answer, "I don't know," I said with tears running down my face. The truth is, I actually knew what I was surviving, but was too ashamed and embarrassed to say it out loud. I was surviving all the trauma I encountered in my youth. I was reliving those years of neglect and under appreciation in my marriages. To me, it was as if I was worthless and unlovable. No matter how hard I tried, I was unable to earn the love and respect I craved. It was at that moment, I realized I was broken, and it was up to me to change the trajectory of my life.

The first step was to truly accept the things I cannot change. There are no do-overs of the past. As the saying goes, "You cannot put the toothpaste back in the tube." I had to take myself out of vic-timhood and start living my life.

The second step was to learn to love myself, to respect myself and to believe in myself. That was truly a difficult step to take, but with hard work I was able to do that. As a homework assignment during one of the sessions I was told to put my arms around myself and say out loud, "Csilla, I love you," before bedtime each night. Although I thought the assignment was silly, I did as I was told. I was good at following directions and doing what others wanted me to do. To my amazement I began feeling better about myself and was able to sleep so much better each night.

The next assignment was equally as strange to me. I was directed to just say, "Thank you," when someone paid me a compliment. In the past, I always made a negative comment to a compliment. To me, a compliment was an offhanded ridicule of what I looked like, or what I was wearing.

With each step I learned to love myself and to believe in myself. I learned that anything is possible regardless of the circumstances if I truly believed. Slowly, I was putting the broken pieces back together.

The final step was to remove the triggers that led to arguments and disappointments in the marriage. This step was extremely hard. I was told to respond with "Yes, you are right," and then walk away or "No, you are wrong," and walk away. By not fueling the fire, the arguments quickly ended. What a huge difference that made in my life and in my marriage.

And, so, my interest in psychology was piqued. I returned to school to pursue a degree in the field. A short two years later I received my M.A. in counseling. I was so proud of myself. That same year my Blake received his B.S. in biology as well. 1995 was a great year!

While at Trevecca Nazarene College, we received information about a doctoral program that was being offered through Southern California University for Professional Studies. This fully accredited program was something we were encouraged to check out. After careful consideration, I said to myself, "Why not?" and I enrolled in the program. A short 3 years later I graduated Magna Cum Laude with my Doctor of Psychology (PsyD) degree. I almost had to pinch myself to make sure what I accomplished wasn't a dream.

I did my internship at Pathfinders, an alcohol and drug treatment center. My experience while working there led me to open my private practice offering outpatient alcohol and drug counseling, domestic violence counseling, parenting classes, and DUI school.

Yes, I was still teaching, and now I had my private practice as well. "Should I continue to do both, or retire from teaching?" is a question I asked myself often. I followed my intuition and decided to do both, since for as long as I can remember, I felt led to be a teacher, and that is exactly what I was doing in both professions. Over the nearly four decades, I touched and helped mold the lives of more than a thousand children under my care, and in my private practice, I helped restore at least as many lives. To this day, because of social media, I have received many testimonials from former students and former clients thanking me for the influence I had on their lives.

Although things were not perfect, things were good and getting better with each passing day. I can truly say I was happy, but just when things were moving in the right direction, tragedy occurred. The school day just started when my phone rang. It was during the national anthem and the moment of silence. Luckily one of my room mothers was in the room at the time so I was able to answer my phone. It was my business partner. He nonchalantly said, "Your husband is dead. He died in a fatal car accident," as if it was just a fender bender. I ran from my classroom in shock, disbelief, and tears heading toward the office. My mind was racing! Oh God, how can this be? Surely this is a terrible mistake! Why was the news coming from him? Where was the police? Why did they not notify me? As I entered the office, the secretary looked up from her work, and as soon as she saw my face, she jumped from her chair, ran to me, and started hugging me. She kept repeating, "I'm so sorry. I'm so sorry." It was at that moment she realized she made a mistake. She told me that the Central Office called her and wanted to know if my classroom was covered since they heard about the fatal accident. She told them that they were mistaken since I was at work and was my usual happy self. As she hung up the telephone, she figured it had to have been a mistake, and with that, she dismissed the call. How could this have happened? Why was I the last to find out about his death? I was his wife. I should have been notified first. Yes, everything was twisted and chaotic that day. When the initial shock wore off, and reality set in, I became numb!

With virtually no one to turn to, I was falling apart on the inside. How did this happen? How do I tell my daughter who was at college in Texas? I couldn't even be there for her. My heart was hurting for her and I could do nothing to comfort her. Once again God gave me an angel named Elaine who was waiting for me at my house. Without her I was virtually paralyzed. She helped me with locating my husband and assisted with all facets of the necessary arrangements. Once my children arrived, she stepped back and allowed them to take over. They, too, gave me the support and help I so desperately needed even though they were also going through the shock and grieving process. His daughters from the first marriage were included in the decision making of the final arrangements as well. I felt this would help them with their dad's passing.

To my surprise, almost all my siblings attended the funeral. It took this tragedy to give me my first glimpse of family unity. I never expected or even thought anyone from my family would show up to support me, but they did. My father, who hardly ever had a decent comment about anything, said that of all the funerals he had attended over the years that was the most impressive. Of course, it was. Since he was a Judicial Commissioner for Wilson County, all the flags were at half staff, and the church was completely full, with many people standing outside since there was no more room inside the church. The funeral procession was led by all the police officers in our town. The funeral was beautiful and helped bring closure for my family.

Lenti and Blake sporting a couple of my hand-painted sweatshirts

Blake receiving his B.S. in 1995, Csilla receiving her M.A. in 1995, and Lenti receiving her B.S. in 2004

Chapter 12

Challenges Continue

Navigating my new life, the life of being a widow, brought many new challenges. Never did I see myself as a widow especially at my age. I was only 52 at the time of his death. I was still dealing with the death of my beloved mother when this tragedy occurred.

As a single mom, dealing with my grief and the grief of my children was nearly unbearable. I was juggling work, parenting and many other issues. Sadly, the truth is, the wall I built to protect myself from brokenness also kept the blessings out. It took years for me to realize that healing didn't mean the damage never existed. It simply meant the damage no longer controlled my life. I was thankful that I found the strength to let go of the past and move forward.

Soon after the funeral, every vulture swarmed in trying to capitalize on the death of my husband. His dear friends, co-workers, some of his own family members, and even my business partner became scavengers. Each one thought there was money to be made from his death, so lawsuits became the norm. Little did they know that he had no money. The small insurance policy barely covered his funeral expenses. There was nothing extra.

My business partner started to embezzle from our practice. He threatened me with physical harm and stalked me day and night. The stalking resulted in me having to flee from my home and eventually selling the house which was my home, and the home of my children for nearly 20 years. Thankfully my dear friend Ron took me in during those scary times and stood by me as I navigated through the chaos.

As if that wasn't enough, my late husband's creditors were ringing the phone off the wall at all hours of the day and night demanding money. Years prior to his death, at the advice of my therapist, we separated our money and finances for reasons mentioned earlier. We had separate accounts in separate banks. I was not a co-signer of any of his loans. I was not legally responsible for his personal debts, overdrawn bank account, or his credit card charges. Of course, that did not stop the continuous harassment from those folks trying to squeeze the last penny I had.

The final lawsuit came from one of the people who was in the car at the time of the accident. I didn't understand why I was being sued. I was not driving the car on that fateful night. I was not there. Why did I have to clean up the mess? I was feeling resentment and frustration. There were times I wanted to throw up my hands and give up, but instead, I chose to dig my heels in and push through it all. My daily chant became, "I can do this."

I hired an amazing team of attorneys who took care of all those matters. Although I was drowning in legal fees, I was thankful for their work on my behalf. I spent four long years in and out of court before everything was resolved, but life was slowly getting back to normal.

I was already working two jobs. I was teaching, had my practice, and now I took on a third job at the airport working on the ramp for American Eagle. It took these three jobs to cover all the legal expenses, plus the expense of my daughter's college tuition (She graduated from Texas A & M in 2004 and a couple of years later received her MA from TCU), and helping my son occasionally when he needed help. As always, I did what had to be done to take care of the financial obligations that were squarely on my shoulders. Often my father's words from long ago came back to me. "You are a Batizy. A Batizy never quits. You will endure and you will be triumphant."

Looking back, I have no idea where the strength came from to get me through those turbulent years following my husband's death. Could it have been my own stubbornness? Was it my father's words that were the driving force that kept me going? Or was it Divine intervention? I choose to believe it was Divine intervention. I, once more, realized that I was blessed beyond belief in all aspects of my life.

2011 Outstanding employee airplane dedication and I'm marshalling in a plane

Chapter 13

My Loves

My children, the loves of my life, were my inspiration, my driving force, and strength throughout my journey. Was I the perfect parent? Absolutely not, but in all decisions, I made, I did the best I knew how to put their well-being first and foremost. Each day, I sought God's guidance in dealing with the challenges of parenthood, and I still pray every day for the well-being of my children. To me, they are still my babies just in adult bodies, which I believe, is typical of most mothers' thinking. They are not only my loves, but they are the greatest blessings in my life.

I taught my children to always be the best they can be, and not to give up no matter what obstacles got in their way. I think I learned the importance of this from my own upbringing, but instead of ridiculing my children, like I was ridiculed and belittled while growing up, I gave my children love and support. I was always proud of their efforts knowing they gave their best. To this day, I never pass up the opportunity to tell them I love them, and that I am proud of them.

Additionally, I taught my children to be kind and loving people. They were taught to help those less fortunate and to volunteer their time through various community services. Some of their volunteer work was through the church, scouting, or at times, simply seeing a person in need and doing what they knew was the right thing to do. They were taught to be givers not takers. I knew both my children understood this life lesson as evidenced by their achievements in this area. Blake earned the rank of Eagle Scout. That honor is attained by only 4% of the boys in scouting. As part of his public service, he painted handicapped parking spaces at retail stores. His sister, Lenti, at age 11 was honored in Washington, D.C. for her community service. While in Washington, D.C., she and 49 other young people had the privilege of dining with the First Lady of the United States.

Both of my children followed their dreams and became accomplished professionals in their chosen fields. My son's passion is in the food industry. In the early years of his career, he was a food innovator developing new products for several nationally known companies. Today, he is the Director of Research for Major Products, Inc. My daughter also followed her dream and has worked in public relations for over a decade. Currently, she is serving as executive vice president of ECPR. I am so proud of the adults they have become.

When my daughter married in 2014, she asked her brother to officiate the ceremony. It was beautiful not just because of the words spoken, but because of the love and family unity that was evident for all to see. It truly warmed my heart to witness the love between my children. Growing up, I only got a few glimpses of family unity. We were too busy trying to survive, or at least I was, to really show love and appreciation for the other siblings. This, obviously, was not the case for my children.

My 3rd love, my first grandchild, Margot Blake, arrived in 2018. She is not only my joy, but the joy of all who are around her. Her smile, laughter, and personality are infectious. When I hold her in my arms, memories of my mother and grandparents come to my mind. It is my desire to give her all the love that I felt from my grandparents, and to have the time to create for her the beautiful memories that I recall of the summers I spent at Nagymami and Nagypapi's house in Gödöllö along with the love and appreciation I felt from Anyu and Valika. It is through their example I learned to be a loving, caring, and doting mother and nagymami.

Blake and Lenti right before the wedding; Blake officiating his sister's wedding

Jeff, Lenti, Blake, Csilla, Lou with Margot Blake

Margot's Lullaby

By: Csilla Smith

Kicsi Baba

Kicsi baba aludjál,
Csukbe a szemend és álmondjál.
Álmondj gyönyörü álmokat,
Kicsi baba aludjál.

Aludjál, aludjál,
Kicsi baba aludjál.
Csukbe a szemed és álmondjál,
Kicsi baba aludjál.

Little Baby

Little baby go to sleep,
Close your eyes and dream some dreams.
Dream beautiful dreams,
Little baby go to sleep.

Sleep, sleep,
Little baby go to sleep.
Close your eyes and dream some dreams,
Little baby go to sleep.

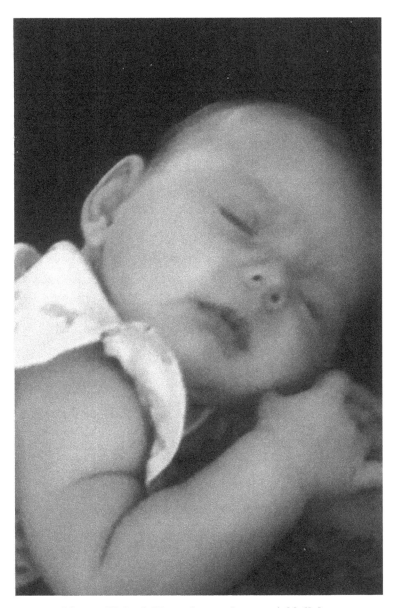

Margot Blake falling asleep to her special lullaby

Margot is a delight to all who know her

Chapter 14

Final Words

My journey is far from over. I look forward to whatever life has in store for me in the future. Meanwhile, I am grateful for the peace I finally found. I am in awe of all the challenges I was able to overcome. These trials started with being taken from my loving home and being thrust into a dysfunctional blended family where parenting skills were lacking. Learning a foreign language, strange customs, and trying to assimilate were yet other struggles I had to overcome. The twists and turns of life were difficult, but through God's grace and love, I was able to maneuver through them all. I thank God for placing all the people who just "happened" in my life at the exact right moment when I had nowhere to go, and in total despair. These people helped me in my journey when I was truly torn and broken.

Recently my brother Levente published his book, The Biggest Hole in the Iron Curtain. He did an amazing job of researching and detailing our father's family history from as far back as the thirteenth century. Likewise, he chronicled portions of our growing up in the United States and gave each of us our own chapter to write our story from youth to adulthood in America.

After reading his book, I realized that there was a huge omission in the story of our growing up in America that remained untold—at least from my perspective. When I wrote my chapter, I was afraid to put in writing my experiences. My voice was once more silenced by fear. I didn't have the courage to put on paper what life was really like for me once I was torn from my home in Hungary.

To my amazement, reading my brother's book opened my eyes. It was the first time I heard about the struggles my siblings endured as well. I had no idea we all suffered, and we were all broken. And it is because of their courage to write about their struggles that I found my voice to tell my story as I lived it.

While my father preached family unity, in reality, he taught us through his actions, family division. He accomplished this division by constantly putting a person down and comparing one child to another. The daily ridicule and name calling never stopped and only caused resentment for the siblings toward each other, along with self-doubt and low self-esteem especially since we were a blended family. Our struggles were real!

Today, I realize that despite our unconventional upbringing, our father always strived for excellence and pushed his children to do the same in every aspect of our lives. As a young child, I never thought or imagined where the money came from for swimming, club memberships, camp, let alone, clothing and feeding 13 children. All these were made possible as a result of my father's work ethic and determination.

Not long ago, my son thanked me and complimented me for the incredible work ethic I instilled in him. Obviously, I learned this from my father. As a young child I saw him work long hours and pick up shifts whenever he could. Through that example, I learned the meaning of hard work and was able to pass that to my children. For this, I am grateful.

At a recent reunion with my family, my youngest sister told me that Dad changed as he got older. She shared with me how, over the years, he had become a gentle, caring father. I wish I could have met that man. I left home at sixteen and for thirteen years after I left, I never spoke to the man. In 1980 we reconnected, and I saw him a handful of times until he passed away in 2007. The father I knew was neither gentle nor caring, but I was happy to hear that the years mellowed him and that some of my siblings along with some of my nieces and nephews got to see that side of him.

Oh, how I longed to hear my father, just once, tell me that he loved me, and that he was proud of me, but those words were never spoken by him while I was growing up. And, as I write these last few words, I close my eyes and the image of that little 8-year-old refugee girl with only the clothes on her back is what I see. Tears pour down my face as I softly whisper, "Csilike, I love you. I'm so proud of you."

BROKEN NO MORE

My family in 2018: Jeff, Margot, Csilla, Blake, Lance, Lenti and my family in 2019: Csilla, Lance, Blake, Jeff, Margot, and Lenti